SYMBOLS

SYMBOLS

A UNIVERSAL LANGUAGE

JOSEPH PIERCY

Michael O'Mara Books Limited

This paperback edition first published in 2017

First published in Great Britain in 2013 by
Michael O'Mara Books Limited
9 Lion Yard
Tremadoc Road
London SW4 7NQ

A CIP catalogue record for this book is available from the British Library.

Papers used by Michael O'Mara Books Limited are natural, recyclable
products made from wood grown in sustainable forests. The manufacturing
processes conform to the environmental regulations of the country of origin.

ISBN: 978-1-78243-000-1 in hardback with jacket print format
ISBN: 978-1-78243-873-1 in hardback print format
ISBN: 978-1-78243-769-7 in paperback print format
ISBN: 978-1-78243-073-5 in ePub format
ISBN: 978-1-78243-072-8 in Mobipocket format

1 2 3 4 5 6 7 8 9 10

www.mombooks.com

Cover design by Ana Bježančević
Designed by Ana Bježančević, typeset by www.glensaville.com

Printed and bound by CPI Group (UK) Ltd,
Croydon, CR0 4YY

For Polly and Joanna

By the same author:

The Story of English
This Book Will Make You Think
(as Alain Stephen)

CONTENTS

INTRODUCTION

'In our thinking we make use of a great variety
of symbol-systems – linguistic, mathematical,
pictorial, musical, ritualistic. Without such symbol-
systems we should have no art, no science, no law,
no philosophy, not so much as the rudiments of
civilization: in other words, we should be animals.'

Aldous Huxley

In his foreword to Jiddu Krishnamurti's philosophical
work *The First and Last Freedom* (1954), the science fiction
novelist Aldous Huxley makes a clear distinction between
the explanatory symbols used in science – 'well chosen,
carefully analysed and progressively adapted' – and those
adopted by religious and political groups for the calculated
exclusion of outsiders. Arguing that such symbols are often
accorded a level of respect they don't deserve, he goes so
far as to say that, 'as the history of our own age makes so
abundantly clear', symbols can even be fatal.

It is important to remember that Huxley was writing in

the aftermath of the Second World War, a period in which political and religious groups had rallied against one another beneath flags and logos of various descriptions, but his point remains just as salient today, as humankind enters a post-industrial era ever more dominated by seismic leaps in technology. New signs, such as the Bluetooth symbol, and new meanings for old signs, such as the Twitter hashtag, are constantly appearing and changing the way in which we communicate with each other about the evolving world in which we live.

But what is it that drives societies and cultures to construct symbol systems in the first place, with all the helpful yet potentially dangerous information they represent? Such systems proliferate today as much as they ever have, but it is only in the last century or so that philosophers, in a dense and often impenetrable field of study, have given considerable thought to what it all means. The Swiss philosopher Ferdinand de Saussure contended that the meaning ascribed to particular signs is, at root, quite arbitrary: the physical symbol has no direct relation to the thing it is meant to represent. It is this disconnect that allows, say, the swastika to be transformed from an ancient symbol of well-being to the insignia of the repressive Nazi party. Anyone presented with a swastika image nowadays perceives a dark and hateful message entirely unrelated to its original meaning, but all the symbol itself really is is a simple geometrical pattern.

The search for meaning behind the 'signifiers' of human existence is intricate and difficult, and to avoid getting too embroiled in the complexity of these theories (and counter-theories) I have included a bibliography and suggestions for further reading at the back of this book. Roland Barthes and Umberto Eco have made particularly interesting additions to Saussure's line of thinking.

Above all, this book is an attempt to look at some of the common (and less common) signs and symbols that we see around us every day, and to trace their historical backgrounds and uses as tools of human communication and understanding. The text is structured thematically, taking as a point of departure elements from earlier civilizations, such as Palaeolithic cave paintings and Ancient Egyptian hieroglyphics. Subsequent sections address more abstract signs and symbols, including familiar political and ideological emblems, symbols relating to concepts of value and exchange, cultural totems of identity and the increasing use of symbols in technology and communication.

The choice of the symbols is arbitrary and miscellaneous – quite pointedly so. There are certainly numerous other signs and symbol systems that merit analysis and study but I have selected those that have had an enduring impact on human society and culture, or which may well prove to be of importance in the future. As technological advances continue to streamline the pace of life, and to bring different cultures and languages closer together, the use of signs and symbols can only become more widespread. While we ought to bear in mind the warnings issued by Aldous Huxley in the mid-twentieth century, it is exciting to see – and speculate on – where our increasing reliance on non-verbal communication will take us.

Joseph Piercy

PART ONE

EARLY SIGNS AND SYMBOLS

'In the rough, a symbol is a sign that
stands for something and something must
exist for the symbol to symbolise.'

Alfred Korzybski

*S*ince the earliest known civilizations, humankind has created signs and symbols. But although we have clear evidence of primitive man's attempts to represent his world through cave paintings and rock art inscriptions, we do not know for certain the motivation behind these creations. Nonetheless, they remain important as a starting point for any examination of the use of signs and symbol systems. Similarly Egyptian hieroglyphics, though in essence a form of alphabet, rely on the use of pictograms to convey semantic meaning and communicate ideas, all of which places them firmly in the realm of the symbolic. Medieval heraldry is also an ideographic system and interesting for its primary purpose as a means of constructing symbolic identities by transposing human characteristics on to animals.

Palaeolithic Cave Art

The oldest surviving evidence of the human capacity to reflect or attempt to record the nature of life and consciousness, and to communicate through visual and symbolic imagery, can be found in Palaeolithic cave art.

In December 1994, three French speleologists (cave explorers) led by Jean-Marie Chauvet were studying geological aspects of the Ardèche valley in southern France when they happened upon a series of interlocking chambers previously hidden by rock falls. The floor of the chambers contained animal bones, prints, fossilized remains and clear evidence of human occupation. As they ventured further into the complex, Chauvet and his colleagues discovered hundreds of well-preserved paintings and engravings on the walls of two vast chambers linked by a short passageway. The first chamber contained images painted mostly in red dyes, whereas the majority of the images in the second chamber were predominantly marked in black charcoal and ochre.

Prehistoric cave paintings were not merely decorative; they also communicated to other hunter-gatherers where dangers or sources of food might be found

The Chauvet Cave paintings are chiefly depictions of animals, with thirteen different species represented in various forms and combinations, including woolly rhinoceroses, cave bears, lions, mammoths, wolves, horses and a large black cat thought to be a panther. For Chauvet, an enthusiastic amateur treasure hunter, the discovery was the culmination of several decades of exploring the caves of the Ardèche region. Realizing the significance of the find, he enlisted the help of archaeologist Jean Clottes, the leading French authority on prehistoric art.

By using modern radiocarbon dating methods, Clottes estimated that the paintings Chauvet and his team had discovered were at least 30,000 to 32,000 years old, making them, at that time, the oldest prehistoric artworks ever uncovered. Of particular interest to Clottes, however, was the level of sophistication in the images and their arrangements and the range of different animals depicted. Up until the discoveries by Chauvet and his team, the abiding theories as to the purpose and function of prehistoric cave paintings had centred on the notion that they were crude, decorative representations of primitive hunter-gatherer experiences; the animals depicted were those over which prehistoric groups traditionally had mastery, either for food or as beasts of burden. But the Ardèche paintings depicted a wide range of animals, many of which, such as lions, rhinos and cave bears, would not have been hunted as prey but rather would have been feared and revered by early humans.

The insides of the cave contained the skeletons of over forty cave bears (a species thought to have become extinct 12,000 years ago) as well as numerous paw prints, scratches and hollows, which suggested to Clottes that the bears had used the caves for hibernation. A particularly fascinating feature in one of the main chambers was evidence of a hearth and a mound of earth on which the skull of one of the bears appeared to have been symbolically placed, as if to create an altar. Clottes came to the conclusion that the two sets of red and black paintings belonged to two distinct periods during which the cave was inhabited by humans, with the majority of the artwork probably created during the Aurignacian culture of broadly 40,000 to 30,000 BC. Subsequent markings, such as scorch marks from torches, additional charcoal embellishments and the perfectly preserved footprint of a young child appeared to date from the later Gravettian period (30,000 to 22,000 BC). It was therefore possible that the original inhabitants (and artists) had abandoned the cave, only for it to be rediscovered by a different tribe some 5,000 years later. This second group of inhabitants, perhaps awed by what they discovered, may have viewed the site as sacred and religious.

Alongside the depiction of various animals were numerous red dots and handprints, the latter made by blowing the pigment around a hand pressed to the wall – a sort of stencil – or by painting the palm with the dye to form a press, very much in the manner of children's nursery-school paintings today. There were no representations of complete human forms, but Clottes singled out the disembodied legs and bison heads as of particular significance. Could it be that the cave was used for quasi-religious rituals and ceremonies, with the minotaur-like figure representing a prehistoric shaman? In an interview in the *Los Angeles Times* in 1995, he outlined his theory as to the social context in which the Chauvet Cave paintings were produced:

> [The] artists came to this cave and found the bear skeletons … Perhaps they were impressed by the skeletons and considered the cave to be full of the bears' spirit, a powerful cave. They may have thought that, by painting some bears and other dangerous animals, they were capturing the animals' spirits, adding power in their own lives.

Following the discovery of the caves, Clottes teamed up with David Lewis-Williams, a renowned South African anthropologist in the study of ancient rock art and a noted champion of the unfashionable view that cave paintings held symbolic value and were not simply arbitrary reflections of everyday experience. The two academics studied the arrangement and style of the different images at Chauvet and other prehistoric rock-art sites in relation to neuropsychological phenomena such as shamanic trance states, and in 1998 published their theories in *The Shamans of Prehistory: Trance and Magic in the Painted Caves*. The book drew comparisons between the practice of shamanism common in many primitive cultures across the world and the theoretical proposition that the caves were used as places of sacred ritual, with the paintings representing powerful symbols key to ceremonial worship. It initially received a mixed reception from the academic community – critics were concerned by the unconventional nature of the theoretical models employed and the use of comparison and conjecture in place of raw evidence – but less sceptical readers, whilst acknowledging the flaws in Clottes and Lewis-Williams' studies, found the central tenet of their argument compelling in its opening up of new areas for intellectual enquiry and debate.

What is without doubt is that the discovery of the Chauvet Cave paintings and the work of Clottes and Lewis-Williams represented a watershed moment in our understanding of prehistoric art, and of early human endeavours to invest meaning in signs and symbols.

The 'Secret' Cave Under the Sea

Prior to the discovery of the Chauvet Cave paintings, the title of Europe's oldest works of art belonged briefly to the Cosquer Cave at the Calanque de Morgiou near Marseille on the French Mediterranean coast.

In September 1985, a professional diving instructor named Henri Cosquer was exploring an underwater cave complex when he found an entrance leading into a long narrow passageway. Cosquer made subsequent explorations of the passageway, venturing a little further into the dark tunnel each time, until eventually he came to a large open chamber. To Cosquer's amazement, the chamber was above sea level and was filled with stunning stalactite formations and aragonite crystals. Cosquer, for reasons that have never been fully explained, decided to keep his discovery to himself, later claiming in a television documentary that he felt it was his 'own secret garden'.

Cosquer's cave did not remain his private

domain for long, however. The Calanque de Morgiou is a popular area for cave divers and in 1991 a team of four amateur divers got lost exploring the same caves. Cosquer was called in to help with the rescue mission, but only one of the divers survived. Realizing the perilous nature of his secret garden might lead to future fatalities, Cosquer revisited the cave with a team of five experienced divers. It was during this second 'unofficial' expedition that he noticed the array of handprints and animal images preserved on the walls and ceiling of the main chamber. Cosquer and his team photographed the interior of the cave and shot video footage as evidence, but their miraculous discovery was at first met with scepticism by scientists, many of whom suspected an elaborate hoax. Experts were particularly perplexed by several images of sea creatures; aside from occasional pictures of fish-like shapes, sea animals had not previously been common in Palaeolithic paintings – not to mention the octopus, penguins and seals that were unique to Cosquer's cave.

The French Ministry of Culture sanctioned further explorations of the cave in 1992 under the joint directorship of Jean Courtin, an expert in cave exploration, the noted prehistorian Jean Clottes, and Cosquer, along with a team of skilled divers. Using radiocarbon dating from samples taken from the cave, the team were able to prove that the paintings were genuine, with some of the handprints dating back at least 27,000 years.

In the intervening years, mindful of the damage done at the caves in Lascaux, France, where the introduction of fresh air and the breath of thousands of visitors caused irreparable damage to the cave paintings, the French government has carefully monitored exposure to the Cosquer Cave, granting only a handful of specialists limited access for research purposes. The major threat to the preservation of the cave images, however, is not from overexposure but from the steadily rising sea level. Just as the caves were first submerged during the thaw at the end of the first ice age, so the acceleration in global warming will eventually wash the paintings away. Perhaps this is why Henri Cosquer felt compelled to keep his discovery a secret.

The Rosetta Stone

Napoleon Bonaparte was a titanic figure in European history, revered as a brilliant military strategist, charismatic general and legal and social reformer. Rather less commonly known is the influence, albeit indirectly, he had on the study of hieroglyphics, the system of signs and symbols used in Ancient Egypt.

In 1798, Napoleon was detailed to undertake an expedition to Egypt. The principal aim of the mission was to establish a significant military foothold in the Middle East, in an attempt to undermine growing British influence in the area. Alongside the invasion forces, Napoleon also assembled teams of experts in various fields such as civil engineering, cartography, history, art and botany, with a view to providing a detailed survey of the landscape, history and culture of Egypt. It is unclear how his interest in Ancient Egypt developed – some scholars have suggested that Napoleon, a man with a notoriously inflated sense of his own power and importance, may have been attracted to the deification of the great rulers of Egypt's distant past and the pomp and grandeur of their temples and tombs – but whatever the reason for his fascination, the teams of experts he assembled made important discoveries that proved invaluable in the field of Egyptology. The surveyors produced the first detailed maps of the tombs in the Valley of the Kings, uncovering several new sites that had hitherto been hidden, and recovered and catalogued over 5,000 ancient treasures and artefacts.

Arguably the most important discovery was that made by accident by a young civil engineer named Pierre Bouchard. Bouchard had been put in charge of rebuilding an old Turkish fortress in the town of Rashid (Rosetta), close to Alexandria. Napoleon wished to establish a strategic military base at the mouth of the Nile Delta – the meeting point of the Nile and the Mediterranean Sea – and he saw Rashid as the perfect location. On 15 July 1799, whilst excavating the foundations of the fort, Bouchard came across a large granite slab covered in carved inscriptions. A highly educated man, he noticed that the inscriptions appeared to be written in three separate forms; intuitively surmising the potential importance of his discovery, he informed Napoleon and his deputy, General Jacques-François Menou.

The Rosetta Stone shows the same proclamation in three different scripts and was crucial in unlocking the mysteries of Egyptian hieroglyphics

Napoleon had recently established a scientific institute to help collate the work of his scholars and surveyors and Bouchard personally transported what had by now been named the Rosetta Stone to Cairo. Copies of the inscriptions were made and sent back to France for further study, and Napoleon viewed the stone in person before returning home himself, leaving Menou in charge of the expedition.

By now the French outposts in Egypt were coming under

increasing threat from military incursions by the British and the Ottoman Turks, and Menou and his troops were forced out of Cairo after losing several key battles. Taking the Rosetta Stone and other artefacts with them, they retreated to Alexandria. With their warships all but destroyed by Lord Nelson during the battle of Abukir Bay, Menou and the remnants of the French expedition were eventually forced to surrender. A protracted argument as to the ownership of the Rosetta Stone and the other French-found items ensued, with the British commander, General Hely-Hutchinson, requisitioning all the materials as spoils of war and Menou claiming they were the property of the French scholars. (According to some contemporary accounts, Menou even claimed that the Rosetta Stone belonged to him as he had been involved in its discovery.) Inevitably, with Menou in a perilous bargaining position given that his remaining troops were effectively stranded in Egypt, the ancient treasures were handed over to the British in exchange for the French scholars' right to retain their original research papers. Colonel Tomkyns Hilgrove Turner was entrusted with the job of transporting the Rosetta Stone back to the United Kingdom, where, on the orders of George III, it was put on display at the British Museum.

Although the Stone had been captured by the British,

the French scholars had made multiple copies of its text while it was in their possession. Meanwhile, the discovery and capture of the Stone, and the work of Napoleon's team in Egypt, had sparked huge public interest across Europe, culminating in a race to be the first to decipher the script; British Egyptologists also made copies and produced plaster casts that were sent to the universities at Oxford, Cambridge and Edinburgh.

It was universally agreed that Pierre Bouchard had been correct to surmise that the inscriptions on the stone were the same proclamation written in three different scripts, and scholars across Europe were able to use the Ancient Greek portion at the bottom to decipher the other two: Ancient Egyptian hieroglyphics at the top and Demotic, another form of Egyptian script, in the middle. It was the work of over two decades, however, with a number of academics making small but significant discoveries that solved another part of the riddle.

The French scholar Antoine Isaac Silvestre de Sacy approached the enigma of the Rosetta Stone by concentrating his research on the Demotic portion, adopting the theory that he could determine its alphabetical structure by matching the names written in Greek with the unknown script. He made some progress by cross-referencing in this way, but fell short of establishing the alphabet. A Swedish scholar, Johan Åkerblad, followed de Sacy's method and was more successful, coming to the conclusion that the Demotic script contained an alphabet of twenty-nine letters, although he was unable to use this discovery to translate the hieroglyphics. It fell to British antiquarian Thomas Young to focus on another of de Sacy's theories: that the hieroglyphic characters might be phonetic representations rather than symbolic ones, as had previously been assumed. He painstakingly compared the proper names across all three versions and discovered several correlations that led him to conclude that they were indeed spelled out phonetically in the hieroglyphics – a breakthrough that still, alas, was no great help in decoding the rest of the sign system.

In 1822, twenty-three years after the discovery of the Stone, a French scholar named Jean-François Champollion uncovered the conclusive last piece of the puzzle – a giant leap forward in the understanding of hieroglyphics. Champollion had been corresponding with other Egyptologists, one of whom, William John Bankes, had discovered and made copies of other inscriptions of names found on Egyptian temples written in Demotic, Greek and hieroglyphic scripts. Bankes sent copies of the inscriptions to Champollion, who compared them with the scripts on the Rosetta Stone and realized that hieroglyphics contained both phonetic and symbolic elements. Through further research, Champollion was able to decipher further names and words from hieroglyphic inscriptions, and in 1824 produced a book containing the first hieroglyphic dictionary and tentative Ancient Egyptian grammar. He was richly rewarded for his discoveries, including being honoured by Louis XVIII of France, who made him a director of the Egyptian museum at the Louvre in Paris.

Champollion's rules enabled Egyptologists to translate thousands of lines of hieroglyphic text, opening up some of the key mysteries of Ancient Egyptian history. The Stone itself is still one of the prime exhibits in the British Museum, where it has been on display for over two centuries.

What Does the Rosetta Stone Actually Say?

The text of the Rosetta Stone, also known as the Memphis Decree, is in essence an agreement between Pharaoh Ptolemy V Epiphanes and the high priests of the Egyptian temples, issued in 196 BC on the anniversary of the pharaoh's coronation. Ptolemy I had been a prominent general under Alexander the Great and succeeded the Warrior King as ruler of Egypt after Alexander's death, beginning a sovereign dynasty that lasted three centuries until the Roman invasion of 30 BC. Ptolemy V Epiphanes ascended the throne during a period of political and social upheaval in Egypt. His father had died suddenly and his mother was murdered in a palace coup, leaving the six-year-old as a pawn in a power battle for control of the country.

Epiphanes' coronation had been delayed for several years due to palace infighting, but after securing the support of the priests he was formally crowned in the ancient city of Memphis – 20 kilometres south of modern-day Cairo – a year before the carving of the Rosetta Stone. The purpose of the Stone was to cement the cult of Epiphanes as a god and divine ruler (a prerequisite for an Egyptian pharaoh), but it also represents a skilful piece of political manoeuvring on the part of the high priests. Under the Ptolemaic dynasty, power had shifted from Memphis to the developing metropolis of Alexandria. Epiphanes needed the continued support of the priests to maintain order and legitimize his right to the throne, so in exchange for their sanction he issued the decree set out on the Rosetta Stone, granting them the right to remain in their spiritual home of Memphis (as opposed to relocating to Alexandria) as well as exemption from a series of taxation laws that had been levied on them by his predecessors.

Heraldic Symbols

One of the most complex and enduring systems of symbols, and certainly one of the richest in terms of allegorical meanings, is the ancient art of heraldry and the composition of coats of arms. The word 'herald' derives from the medieval Germanic *harja-waldaz*, which roughly translates as 'army commander'. Originally the job of the herald was to act as a messenger between opposing military factions, and to carry out this duty effectively they needed to be easily identifiable on the field of battle. As military equipment developed – and in particular the increasingly sophisticated forms of armour – the need to identify the allegiance of different military groups became paramount.

By the twelfth century, heralds were also being used as masters of ceremony in medieval tournaments, announcing and introducing the competitors and adjudicating on their birthrights and genealogy. Over time the responsibilities of heralds were increased once more – this time to the status of *nobilitas minor* (minor nobility), on a par with knights and baronets – with the power to grant, record and officiate on coats of arms.

The royal coat of arms of the United Kingdom has as its two *supporters* a rampant lion and the mythical unicorn; the French motto, *'honi soit qui mal y pense'*, means 'shamed be he who thinks evil of it'

The main element of a coat of arms, naturally, given its principal function as a means of identification on the field of battle, is the *escutcheon*: a shield-like shape. This is traditionally divided into sections and decorated with a variety of colourful shapes known as *ordinaries*. Familiar ordinaries include crosses of different styles, horizontal and diagonal sashes, vertical stripes, arrowheads and single circles.

The vertical sash or thick stripe running diagonally from the top left to the bottom right of a shield is known as a *bend*; if used in the reverse direction it is declared a *bend sinister*. Bends are common on the shields of soldiers, as the sash represents the *baldric* – a military shoulder sash – and the ladders used to scale castle ramparts during sieges. Crosses proved particularly popular, with heraldic records and dictionaries recognizing over 100 crucifix variations dating back to the early Crusades at the end of the eleventh century. Other notable ordinaries have more oblique meanings, including the arrowhead shape (or *chevron* in heraldic terms), which is generally taken to signify protection and commonly used on modern military and police uniforms as a designation of rank and status. Circular shapes, known as *roundels*, were technically deemed *sub-ordinaries* and usually represented persons of lesser importance, although roundels were nonetheless granted to families who, despite their lowly standing, were considered loyal and trustworthy.

Each ordinary was usually given a symbolic colour, the names of which derive in the main from Old French but were adopted into English heraldic terminology by the fifteenth century. The classical colours are *sable* (black, denoting grief and prudence), *azure* (blue: honesty and fidelity), *gules* (red: fortitude and resilience), and *vert* (green: love and joy). Gold and purple were often used to represent royal houses as well as glory and lawfulness.

In addition to an ordinary, many escutcheons also contained emblems or, in heraldic terms, *charges*: images of objects and animals. Lions and leopards, traditional symbols of power and valour in battle, are common in medieval heraldic iconography; books naturally represent wisdom and learning, and dogs faithfulness and loyalty. But the complexity of heraldry can be found in the *attitude* of the animal depicted, of which there are seemingly endless combinations, each with its own traditional association. So while a lion may seem a fairly straightforward symbol of bravery, the icon can also convey a number of secondary meanings. A *passant* lion, for instance, shown walking with a raised forepaw, symbolizes an attitude of resolve and perseverance; should the lion be depicted stationary and seated, however, with its head turned towards the observer in a *gardant* position, the beast is reflecting an attitude of prudence and wisdom; a *rampant* lion, rearing on its hind legs, denotes courage.

Full heraldic coats of arms tend to contain a decorated escutcheon along with a combination of other common elements: perhaps a crest, a helmet (in traditional military coats of arms), a motto or *supporters* – two figures placed on either side of the escutcheon, as if holding the shield upright. The royal coat of arms of the United Kingdom has on one side a rampant gardant lion (that is, a rearing beast of prey facing forwards) and on the other the mythical unicorn.

Coats of arms, once granted, are recorded in an official registry such as the College of Arms in London. Each new coat of arms is given a description known as a *blazon*. As an example of the bewildering complexity of the meta-language surrounding heraldry and its conventions, below is the official blazon for the royal coat of arms of the United Kingdom:

> Quarterly, first and fourth Gules three lions passant gardant in pale Or armed and langued Azure (for England), second quarter Or a lion rampant within a double tressure flory-counter-flory Gules (for Scotland), third quarter Azure a harp Or stringed Argent (for Ireland), the whole surrounded by the Garter; for a Crest, upon the Royal helm the imperial crown Proper, thereon

a lion statant gardant Or imperially crowned Proper; Mantling Or and ermine; for Supporters, dexter a lion rampant gardant Or crowned as the Crest, sinister a unicorn Argent armed, crined and unguled Proper, gorged with a coronet Or composed of crosses patée and fleurs de lis a chain affixed thereto passing between the forelegs and reflexed over the back also Or. Motto 'Dieu et mon Droit' in the compartment below the shield, with the Union rose, shamrock and thistle engrafted on the same stem.

Oxford v Cambridge: Coats of Arms

The rivalry between the United Kingdom's two pre-eminent seats of learning, the universities of Oxford and Cambridge, is a long and colourful tradition dating back many hundreds of years. The annual 'Varsity' sporting contests in disciplines such as cricket, rugby and football are fiercely competitive, though none more so than the annual Boat Race on the Thames. The two sides are fairly evenly matched on track, field and river, but one area in which Cambridge has the distinct upper hand is in its city's coat of arms.

The coat of arms for Cambridge, granted in 1575, is elegant and graceful in its design. The escutcheon depicts the name of the city in the form of a *rebus* (picture riddle) showing a bridge traversing the River Cam, with traditional royal symbols of the fleur-de-lys and the Tudor rose. The crest is in the form of Cambridge Castle, a Norman fortification built by William I of which very little now remains, and the arms are flanked by gilded seahorses as supporters. The elements and colours combine and complement each other, creating a gracefully simple design.

In contrast, the coat of arms for the city of Oxford, granted nine years before that of Cambridge, is cluttered and bizarre. Although, like Cambridge, the escutcheon contains a simple rebus spelling out the name of the city – an ox crossing a ford in a river – the crest depicts a blue lion (blue?) in a rampant gardant attitude, holding a Tudor rose while wearing a crown. On either side of the escutcheon are the traditional two supporters: on the right a rampant blue elephant (again, blue?) in chains, who appears to be dressed in pyjamas, and on the left a rearing, evil-looking green beaver, also in manacles. Elizabeth I granted the arms during a royal visit in 1566, and the two supporters are thought to represent two prominent members of her court: Sir Francis Knollys, Lord Lieutenant and High Steward of Oxford (elephant) and Henry Norreys of Rycote, captain of the Oxford militia (beaver). There is no evidence to suggest that Elizabeth chose the design herself, although if she did she clearly had quite a sense of humour. The coat of arms is footnoted with the Latin motto *Fortis est Veritas*, meaning 'The Truth is Strong'. Quite so, Elizabeth, quite so.

The Fleur-de-lys

The fleur-de-lys, or 'flower of the lily', is a symbol common in medieval heraldry and particularly prominent on French coats of arms. The symbol comes in a variety of forms, and though commonly associated with France is comparable with strikingly similar designs dating back to ancient Mesopotamian and Egyptian artworks and decorations.

The symbol itself is generally thought to be a stylized representation of a flowering lily, on the grounds that the side petals fall away from the central crown of the plant. There are, however, some scholars and botanists who dispute that the design is derived from the lily, despite its common name, claiming that it instead represents the iris. The basis for this hypothesis lies in the symbol's adoption as one of the royal symbols of the Frankish kings of France, who were descended from a nomadic Germanic tribe that settled for a time around the iris-banked River Luts in the Netherlands. Proponents of this theory believe that *fleur de Luts* ('flower of the Luts') changed over time to *fleur de lys*, thus causing confusion with the lily.

Whatever its botanic origin, the symbol came to be adopted on the coat of arms of the French monarchy, nowadays having a particular association with the early-ninth-century emperor Charlemagne. The original royal coat of arms consisted of a blue shield scattered with golden fleur-de-lys, but by the reign of Charles V in the late fourteenth century the design had been streamlined to depict just three large symbols. The two differing designs are known in heraldry as France Ancient and France Modern.

King Edward III adopted the fleur-de-lys as a part of English heraldry around the start of the Hundred Years' War in 1337, combining the France Ancient design into the Plantagenet coat of arms as a way of laying claim to the French throne. English monarchs continued to incorporate the symbol in heraldic representations up until the early nineteenth century, while in France the France Modern was replaced as royal standard by the tricolour following the French Revolution of 1789. Nonetheless the fleur-de-lys remains prevalent on flags in regions with a strong French influence, such as Quebec in Canada and New Orleans in the United States.

New Orleans Saints quarterback Drew Brees wears the team's logo, the fleur-de-lys, in an American football game in October 2011

In early Christian iconography the innocent lily was sometimes used in representations of an infant Jesus Christ, but by the thirteenth century scriptures and religious texts were primarily using the flower as a symbol of purity and chastity – and, by extension, the Virgin Mary – although the three flowers of the fleur-de-lys have also been seen as a symbol of the Holy Trinity, with the binding bar across the bottom representing Mary. As well as appearing in paintings and on stained-glass windows featuring the Virgin Mary, it has also been used on the heraldic arms of several popes and cardinals, and it is possible that the adoption of the fleur-de-lys by the early Frankish kings was symbolic of the divine right of monarchs and the spiritual protection bestowed upon them by God.

The modern usage of the fleur-de-lys is widespread and varied. A version of the emblem was incorporated into the logo of the Scout Movement by its founder Robert Baden-Powell, who borrowed the symbol from a military badge given to British Army reconnaissance experts. The fleur-de-lys has also been used as an insignia by other military organizations including the now-defunct Canadian Expeditionary Force, who fought in the Battle of the Somme, as well as the Israeli Intelligence Corps. Thanks to the flower's appearance on the coats of arms of Florence, Italy and New Orleans, it also features on the official colours of Italian Serie A football team ACF Fiorentina and NFL American football team the New Orleans Saints.

Hurricane Katrina and the Symbol of Solidarity

When Hurricane Katrina struck the southern United States in August 2005, New Orleans bore the brunt of the disaster. Eighty per cent of the city was under water due to breaches of the city's levee flood defences and almost 1,500 people lost their lives in New Orleans alone, with tens of thousands of others rendered homeless by the devastation.

Many of the homeless found temporary shelter in the Superdome, home of the New Orleans Saints. At one point it was estimated that the American football stadium was providing sanctuary for up to 20,000 refugees, despite itself suffering severe damage during the storm. The Superdome and the plight of its temporary inhabitants came to symbolize the resilience and determination of the people of New Orleans in the face of adversity. In the aftermath of Hurricane Katrina, many survivors had tattoos designed, inscribed with the date the disaster struck, 8/29, above the symbol of New

Orleans, the fleur-de-lys, to honour the dead and show solidarity with, and fortitude for, the city's rebirth.

PART TWO

SYMBOLS OF IDEOLOGY, IDENTITY AND BELONGING

'In a symbol there is concealment and yet revelation: here, therefore, by silence and by speech acting together, comes a double significance. In the symbol proper, what we can call a symbol, there is ever, more or less distinctly and directly, some embodiment and revelation of the Infinite; the Infinite is made to blend itself with the Finite, to stand visible, and as it were, attainable there. By symbols, accordingly, is man guided and commanded, made happy, made wretched.'

Thomas Carlyle

This section is concerned with some commonly identifiable symbols that, for better or worse, have become associated with human ideologies and identities. Although many such symbols, among them the swastika and the hammer and sickle, have firmly entrenched historical associations, their origins are not always so clear-cut.

Other dominant symbols from modern popular culture, such as the smiley face and the heart, have likewise travelled some distance from their conception and original meaning. It is entirely possible that these symbols will be reappropriated and redefined by future generations and cultures, to suit the changing nature of human expression.

Yin and Yang

The yin and yang, or yin-yang, symbol, also known as the *Taijitu*, originates from the Chinese Taoist tradition. This iconic image consists of a circle divided into two teardrop-shaped halves, one white and one black, each containing a small dot of the opposite colour. In Taoist teachings this eternal, swirling circle of opposites signifies Tao, the unity of all things in the natural and spiritual worlds; the fusion of light and dark is taken to represent the co-dependence of opposite forces. Yin, the dark side, is the feminine side and signifies coldness and passivity, the moon and the night. Yang, the light side, is masculine and reflects heat, action and movement, the sun and the day. The dots show how each pairing of opposing forces cannot exist without recourse to the other; this interrelationship is essential for balance and harmony.

The yin and yang symbol has become absorbed into popular culture, with the central philosophy of maintaining a harmony of opposites extended into areas such as health, healing and diet, and a good work–life balance. The philosophy is also key to the art of Chinese cooking: a single dish or a meal, in order to be fully accomplished, must contain a balance of flavours and ingredients. In this respect, yin and yang are represented by warming or heating properties such as spice (yang foods) and cooling and calming properties such as fruit and vegetables (yin foods). From a nutritional point of view, yang is represented by carbohydrates and yin by vitamins and minerals.

The philosophy behind yin and yang – the co-dependence of opposing forces – has modern-day applications in everything from Chinese cooking to feng shui

Yin and yang is thought to have been inspired by the teachings of Confucius and his natural allegories such as the light and dark sides of a mountain. Perhaps he was merely expressing, in poetic form, an elegant view of the universe and our existence rather than an all-encompassing ethos by which to live, but yin and yang, for better or for worse, has often been appropriated by Western New Age philosophy, particularly self-help and alternative lifestyle theories. In principle, the notion that problems or dilemmas arise from the discord between opposing forces, although simplistic, is a sound enough premise. Where the application of yin and yang to modern-day situations becomes murky is in the methods through which harmony is sought.

Three Major Religions and Their Symbols

The Christian Cross

The Christian cross is one of the most paradoxical symbols in human history, representing at once the death of Jesus Christ and also his glorious resurrection. It serves to remind Christians of both suffering and hope.

Simple crosses of various forms appear repeatedly in the history of symbols, and certainly the cross we now know as Christian existed long before the crucifixion of Christ; its ancient relatives include the Egyptian ankh and the original swastika. Even after the crucifixion it took three centuries for the cross to be openly adopted by Christians: it was only once Emperor Constantine I – the first Roman emperor to convert to Christianity – had abolished crucifixion in AD 337, out of respect for the suffering of Christ, that the cross went from being an instrument of torture to an acceptable symbol of worship.

The crucifix, a three-dimensional representation of Christ on the cross (from the Latin *cruci fixus*, 'fixed to a cross'), is not thought to have arrived until the sixth century AD.

The Star and Crescent

Unlike most religions, Islam does not have an official symbol as such, in keeping with its opposition to religious icons and representations. There are, however, a number of visual images traditionally associated with Islam, including the colour green (which features prominently in the Quran) and the word 'Allah' in Arabic script, though perhaps the best-known Islamic symbol is the star and crescent.

Much like the Christian cross, the star and crescent came into existence long before the religion with which it is now associated. Artefacts indicate that the symbol was important to the ancient Moabite, Sumerian, Parthian and Babylonian civilizations, all based in what we now call the Middle East; in Sumerian mythology, which dates back as far as the fourth millennium BC, the crescent represented the moon god and the star the goddess of love and fertility. By Roman times the symbol had a particular association with Byzantium, modern-day Istanbul, and in the fourteenth century it was in use on the flags of Muslim armies during the Crusades.

The crescent featured on the flag of the Ottoman

Empire from 1453 until its dissolution in 1923, with the star only added in the nineteenth century, and the full symbol still appears on a number of modern-day national flags in predominantly Muslim countries, including Turkey, Pakistan, Algeria and Libya.

The Star of David

The Star of David – a six-pointed star, or hexagram – has only been widely used as a symbol of the Jewish faith since the seventeenth century, although it had been used by certain Jewish communities for around six centuries prior to that. Stars, like crosses, crop up often in religious symbology, and likewise can have wildly different meanings – the pentagram, or five-pointed star, is traditionally associated with either freemasonry or paganism.

The Star of David derives from the medieval idea of the Shield of David – another name for God – which is known to have appeared on a flag used by the Jewish community of Prague in the fourteenth century, and it is also closely related to the Seal of Solomon, a hexagram inside a circle, which featured on the same flag. In 1930s Germany the Star of David became a symbol of persecution, with all Jews forced to wear it, although it was proudly reclaimed after the Second World War as the central symbol on the flag of Israel.

The Star of David has often been used as a symbol of oppression, such as these anti-Semitic clothing badges forced upon millions of Jews in the 1930s and 1940s

The Heart

The heart is a vital symbol in many cultures and belief systems across the world. It is central to religious iconography throughout the ages and is the abiding image of true love on Valentine's Day cards, as well as appearing prolifically on everything from playing cards to 'I ♥ NY' T-shirts. It even has its own electronic communication shorthand: <3. But as anyone with even a passing understanding of human biology knows, the image of the bulging, blood-red heart is anatomically flawed, bearing only a vague resemblance to the actual organ we all have inside us. Why?

One explanation takes us back to the iconography of the Ancient Egyptians, who represented the heart hieroglyphically as a vase-like shape with short protruding handles to represent the arteries and veins. They placed the heart at the centre of both physical and spiritual well-being, leaving it inside the body of a deceased person despite removing all other vital organs during mummification. The reason for this was their belief that the heart would be used by the gods to determine a person's fate in the afterlife: in order to enter Paradise and the Fields of Peace, the deceased would be led by Anubis, guardian of the underworld, to the Hall of Ma'at, which contained the sacred scales of justice upon which the person's heart would be weighed against a feather. If virtuous, righteous and pure, the heart would weigh exactly the same as the feather. But at the foot of the scales sat Ammut, Ma'at's pet, represented in Egyptian iconography as a fearsome dog-like demon; any heart weighed down by its own falsehood and sin would be fed to the hungry beast.

Likewise, albeit minus the ravenous carnivore, many of the world's other religions align the heart closely with the kingdom of the divine. In Judaism it is linked symbolically with the Holy of Holies, the heart of the Temple of Jerusalem where the Ark of the Covenant – by extension the heart of the Jewish faith – was supposed to have been stored. The heart is also common in Christian iconography, notably the concept of the Sacred Heart: the heart of Jesus, representing his love for humanity. Paintings and stained-glass windows from the Middle Ages depict the Sacred Heart encased either in thorns or chains, surrounded by an effervescent golden glow and positioned beneath the sign of the cross. The Catholic Church dates the origin of this image – a forerunner of the modern Valentine's heart – to the visions of Saint Marguerite-Marie Alacoque, a seventeenth-century French nun who received visitations from Jesus in which he told her to rest her head upon his heart so that she might learn his goodliness and devotion.

A stained-glass window depicting the Sacret Heart of Jesus

Religion aside, the classic heart-shaped image we are all familiar with began appearing on decks of French playing cards as early as the 1400s. That said, the heart as a symbol of true love on cards and letters is very much a product of Victorian England, despite Valentine's messages having been exchanged between loves since the Middle Ages.

There remains some debate as to the true origin of the heart as a romantic symbol. Some scholars have argued that the now-extinct Silphium plant, widely used by our ancient ancestors for medicinal purposes – including, significantly, birth control – had heart-shaped seeds. The link between the heart shape and the act of lovemaking is further reinforced by heart-shaped symbols found above the doorways of brothels in the ill-fated city of Pompeii. It is conceivable, therefore, that the use of the heart to signify love and passion may have been popularized in the repressive Victorian era as a coy representation of sexual lust.

I ♥ NY

One of the most distinctive and easily recognized uses of the heart symbol can be found on the logo of tourist souvenirs in New York City. This classic design, a modern-day rebus, is comprised of the letter I and a heart shape, with the initials NY blocked beneath in a classic font known as American Typewriter.

The 'I ♥ NY' logo has gone from a marketing slogan to a much-loved symbol of solidarity

Following the New York blackout of July 1977, which resulted in widespread looting and rioting across the city, William S. Doyle, deputy leader of the New York Department of Commerce, hit upon a plan to get the city to pull together and promote a positive image. Doyle hired Wells Rich Greene to devise a marketing campaign, not just for the city but for New York State as a whole. Wells Rich Greene enlisted the talents of Milton Glaser, a New York-born and bred graphic designer, to devise a logo for their campaign. Glaser took inspiration for his iconic design from car bumper stickers promoting a Montreal radio station he had seen whilst on holiday in Canada. Glaser knew that New York, too, was a 'city with a heart'.

His design proved to be an instant success and quickly began appearing on the now-classic white T-shirts and other memorabilia. It has proved to be an enduring symbol of the city, equal in the popular imagination with the Statue of Liberty or the Empire State Building. Milton Glaser's original design sketches and presentation boards are on permanent display in New York's Museum of Modern Art.

In the aftermath of 9/11, New York once again found itself in need of a symbol of unity and strength in the face of adversity. Glaser produced a new version of his logo, reprising the original I ♥ NY image but adding the words 'More Than Ever' and a small black spot on the red heart.

The Swastika

The swastika, one of the most controversial icons of recent human history, is in fact an ancient symbol that has been used for over 3,000 years: artifacts such as pottery and coins from the ancient city of Troy (in modern-day Turkey) show that it was commonly used as far back as 1000 BC. Gradually it was adopted by many cultures around the world, including Chinese, Japanese, Indian, Native American and European, variously representing the sun, thunder, the Christian cross and alchemy.

The symbol has especially strong links with Southeast Asia, where, among its many iterations, it has been largely seen as a good luck charm and its usage, only slightly muted by political events elsewhere, continues to this day in the Hindu, Buddhist and Jain religions.

Of course, the swastika is most notorious in modern

Western culture for its unalterable connection with Adolf
Hitler's Nazi party and the associated horrors of the Second
World War. Some historians have tried to reclaim it for
posterity and older uses of the symbol have been steadfast
in the face of the dominant Nazi link – it still, to this day,
forms part of the Finnish presidential emblem – but even
variations on the theme, such as three- or five-armed
versions, have effectively been tarnished by association with
the 'classic' four-armed swastika. Inevitably the symbol and
others inspired by it have gleefully been adapted by far-right
extremist factions, such as Eugène Terre'Blanche's Afrikaner
Resistance Movement in South Africa.

A decorative swastika in the garden of the Buddhist Western Monastery in Hong Kong

A Third Reich postage stamp from 1943, showing the Nazis' appropriation of the swastika for a regime far removed from the symbol's original meaning

The Second World War is recent enough to remain a pivotal event in our cultural awareness and the swastika its most powerful and horrifying symbol, but its ability to stir and galvanize vociferous nationalist sentiment predates Hitler's rise to power in the 1930s. In the nineteenth century, for instance, countries around Germany were growing ever larger and forming vast empires, yet Germany itself remained a loose confederation of states until 1871. To counter the feeling of vulnerability and instil a sense of cultural unity, mid-century German nationalists, encouraged by archaeologists making tenuous leaps of faith largely to satisfy racial and ideological fashions for a 'pure-raced' Indo-European ancestry, began to use the symbol as a sign of Germanic superiority. Certainly by the end of the nineteenth century, the swastika could be found on periodicals of the *völkisch* movement, a sort of romanticized German nationalism. Before long it was a prevalent symbol of German nationalism and could be found in a multitude of places, from the emblem of the *Wandervögel*, a German youth movement, to the emblem of the German Gymnasts' League; adorning Lanz von Liebenfels' anti-Semitic periodical *Ostara*; on the arms of various *Freikorps* units; and as a logo of the Thule Society, a supposed 'study group for German antiquity' with decidedly occultist leanings.

It was only really at the outbreak of the Second World War that the swastika accrued its now-familiar evil implications. Indeed, Pathé newsreel from Britain and America in the late 1930s betrays a certain admiration of the majesty and order that was being presented by Germany at the time, and the swastika was the buckle that held it together. It seems inconceivable now that Hitler was *Time* magazine's Man of the Year for 1938. But, originally at least, the German swastika, along with the Nazi salute, identified a resurgent nation but was arguably considered no more brutal than the Union Jack might have been throughout the Indian subcontinent.

Why was it chosen, though? Why the ancient swastika rather than a circle, a dove, or something doodled on a Hitler Post-it note or culled with retrospective meaning from the margin of the first draft of *Mein Kampf*? In fact, Hitler does devote some space in *Mein Kampf* to musing on the choice of symbol, although he credits one Dr Friedrich Krohn, a dentist and Thule Society member, with suggesting to him the eventual design, while geopolitician Karl Haushofer inspired Hitler to imbue it with new meaning and historic 'authenticity'. The classic colour scheme was, and still is, typically Germanic: the white representing nationalism and the red the social aspect of the new dogma. The cross itself was to represent the struggle.

In untangling Hitler's adoption of the swastika, however, it is necessary to dismiss the retroactive and highly speculative nonsense that accompanies all things Nazi. For example, it has been claimed that Hitlerite Unity Mitford gave the Führer the idea for the symbol as her father spent years in the Canadian mining town of Swastika, but the dates simply do not correlate. A more plausible theory is that Hitler's receptiveness to adopting the symbol stemmed, in part, from half-forgotten memories of the monastery in Lambach, Austria, which he attended in his youth and which had swastikas – still visible today – chiselled into its baroque features courtesy of its abbot, Theoderich Hagn, who had spent some time on a religious pilgrimage in the Far East. Abbot Hagn also inscribed both his and the abbey's initials around the building – THLA – from which some theorists have derived portents involving the A and the H but conveniently leaving the other letters alone.

What the symbol nowadays implies, or how acceptable it is, depends largely of course on its context. It is essentially a geometric form – one that might have been doodled from time immemorial by bored cavemen or even more bored schoolboys, and as such the patent is lost to antiquity. Technically speaking it is an irregular icosagen, or twenty-sided polygon, but its implied meaning varies according to the angle of rotation, direction of implied rotation and the direction of each 'hook' (*saustika*). The 'classic' Nazi symbol is generally rotated through 45 degrees, seemingly for aesthetic reasons only. It is cold and sharp and the colouring, as mentioned, is traditionally Teutonic – very different from the crimson daubing one might find on the forehead of a Hindu teenager in India during Diwali in order to invoke good luck, or at the foot of a stained-glass window in Britain, where the symbol is more commonly known as a fylfot.

Some cultures have historically differentiated between the clockwise swastika and the counterclockwise *sauvastika*: the swastika symbolizing health and vitality and the sauvastika meaning bad luck or misfortune. Since the Nazis' use of the swastika there has been a renewed attempt to distinguish between the two 'directions' of the symbol: the clockwise, Nazi version means hate and death while the counterclockwise version retains the symbol's ancient meaning of life and good luck.

As a matter of public law, post-war German law codes prohibit the display of a swastika in any form or fashion, even if used satirically or as part of an anti-Nazi political statement. Even consumer products such as T-shirts and bumper stickers can be confiscated if they contain any depiction of the symbol. While many Germans equate the display of the swastika with the display of the Confederate flag in the United States, others are wary of the effective whitewashing of a dark but grimly significant period in the country's history, arguing that the acknowledgement of a symbol of evil can be the key to diminishing its power.

The Curious Incident of the First World War Bond Scheme

The itinerant nature of the swastika prior to the Second World War is illustrated somewhat ironically by the fact that the British National Savings Committee used a swastika as the symbol for a war bond scheme during the First World War. Contributions would be rewarded with swastika stamps to be stuck onto a coupon, some of which are so well preserved that they can go for up to £200 on eBay. At the same time numerous war bond posters of the period displayed images of uniquely British war sentimentality about helping the elderly and disadvantaged alongside what to the modern eye is undoubtedly a Nazi insignia. They are easy to source but curious to behold, seemingly juxtaposing the detested swastika with a portrait of a dear old granny as she sits in her rocking chair, knitting for the troops.

The Hammer and Sickle

Alongside the swastika and the peace symbol, the hammer and sickle was one of the most enduring political and ideological symbols of the twentieth century. But unlike those two symbols, the origins of the design and especially the identity of its designer remain uncertain.

It seems likely that the hammer and sickle was an adaptation of an earlier symbol of a hammer crossed over a plough that had historically featured in provincial Russian heraldry prior to the Bolshevik Revolution of 1917. Peter the Great had begun instituting grants for the registering of coats of arms in the late seventeenth century, as part of his programme of dragging Russia into line with Western European powers, although the system remained relatively unregulated and ill-defined. It did, however, spawn the coat of arms of Peter the Great's dynasty, the Romanovs, whose distinctive two-headed eagle became the standard symbol of Imperial Russia for the next two centuries.

But following the revolution of 1917, the Bolsheviks were faced with a dilemma: what to do with the ubiquitous symbols of the imperial regime? In the final days of the revolution it had become common practice for overzealous mobs to tear down imperial iconography, smash statues of past monarchs, loot museums and palaces and rip plaques and coats of arms from the doors and walls of state institutions. The newly appointed Commissar of Enlightenment, the writer and revolutionary Anatoly Lunacharsky, became dismayed at the wholesale vandalism of state monuments and lobbied new leader Vladimir Lenin to take measures to curb the destruction. Lunacharsky had been educated in the West, and although he held strong Marxist revolutionary ideals he was a cultured man, well versed in the arts, and he abhorred the violence being committed against the artistic and architectural achievements of Russia's imperial past.

Lenin duly initiated the 'Monumental Propaganda' plan to have the fallen statues systematically replaced with monuments and statues celebrating social and political radicals and the heroes of the revolution. In places where the double-headed eagle had previously hung, the Communist five-point star began to appear.

In 1918, Lunacharsky, on Lenin's advice, opened a competition for artists and designers to create new symbols for the new Russia. The competition was to design a flag, coat of arms and an official state seal. The competition rules stated that 'in the composition there must be elements symbolizing the workers' and peasants' republic – the tools of their work'.

The hammer and sickle of the USSR flag was symbolic not just of a nation but also of the Eastern Bloc's Cold War-era defiance of the West. Here the flag flies proudly behind a portrait of spaceman Yuri Gagarin on a 1963 Romanian stamp

The following year the Council of People's Commissars convened to consider the submissions. The original winning design comprised the rays of light of a rising sun upon a red background, surrounded by sheaves of wheat, with a crossed hammer and sickle in the centre and an upward-pointing sword beneath them. Lenin, though, had second thoughts about the sword and this was swiftly removed when the seal was refined. The key component of the new state seal was the hammer and sickle – in Russian the combination is reversed as 'sickle and hammer' – which perfectly satisfied the criteria Lenin and Lunacharsky had laid down for the competition: the working-class urban proletariat was represented by the hammer and the rural peasant by the sickle.

The emblem was quickly adopted into Bolshevik propaganda and featured heavily in the banners and street art produced for the 1919 May Day celebrations. The hammer and sickle eventually replaced all the symbols of the old regime, appearing on all state documents, currency and regalia. It was adopted as the official flag of the Soviet Union in 1923, and remained until the dissolution of the Soviet Union in 1991.

The question as to the 'authorship' of the flag remains unclear. Various candidates have been promoted by historians, all artists known to have had strong links with the early Bolshevik regime after the revolution, including Sergey Chekhonin, a graphic artist and ceramicist; Evgeny Kamzolkin, a painter in the social realist tradition turned street artist and stage designer; and the sculptor Nikolay Andreyev, who created many of the statues for Lenin's Monumental Propaganda programme. As there is no conclusive evidence to argue for one single designer of the hammer and sickle emblem it seems most likely that it was created and refined by a committee of artists under the direction of Lenin and Lunacharsky.

In the post-Soviet era, the symbol of the hammer and sickle has become tainted as representative of a totalitarian regime and the worst excesses of Communism, and although it is still used as a symbol of the workers' revolution in some parts of the world (notably China), it is more likely to be found on pseudo-nostalgic fashion items such as T-shirts, badges and baseball caps worn by people with little understanding of or sympathy for the revolutionary theories of Karl Marx and Friedrich Engels.

African Variations of the Hammer and Sickle

The use of the hammer and sickle as a representation of the struggle of the workers has been adopted and adapted by other countries with Communist or Communist-inspired regimes, notably in parts of Africa. The flag of Angola, for example, uses the crossed emblems of a machete, to symbolize the rural farmers, and a crescent-shaped cogwheel to represent urban factory workers. In a sinister departure from the convention of using workers' implements and tools as symbols, the flag of Mozambique features an agricultural hoe crossed with an AK-47 rifle and bayonet, with a yellow Marxist-style five-point star as a background. The flag of the People's Republic of the Congo reflected a more traditional approach, however, with a hammer and hoe set inside a wreath on a red Communist-style background, but following the overthrow of the Marxist–Leninist government in 1991, the newly styled Republic of the Congo has adopted a simpler three-striped flag.

The Shamrock and the Four-Leaf Clover

The three-leaf clover, or shamrock, has traditionally been linked with St Patrick and, by association, with Ireland. According to some legends St Patrick used the leaf as a metaphor for the Christian trinity, although the legends in question only seem to date back to the early eighteenth century. The three protrusions may also be symbolic of the three theological virtues found in 1 Corinthians 13:13: faith, hope and love. The spiritual associations of the shamrock predate St Patrick by some time.

Ancient Celts also revered the clover because of the trinity of its leaves. They had a deep understanding of their connection with nature, as well as a myriad of powerful religious and scientific beliefs based on triads, as we see in designs such as the triskelion, the triple spiral, the triqueta, Druid marks and various examples of Celtic knotwork. On a more mundane level, the clover was seen as a substantial food source for livestock – clover growth is prolific with very little provocation – and the Druids considered its impressive vitality a sign of sacredness. In this way, the shamrock came to represent life itself.

The shamrock has only been associated with St Patrick since the early eighteenth century, but it is now a common sight in Ireland, such as on these ornate Dublin streetlamps

The word 'shamrock' is derived from the Irish *seamrog* (summer plant), which is the diminutive version of the Irish word for clover (*seamair*). Irish legends about the shamrock reference a variety of mystical powers: its leaves are said to stand on end to warn of an approaching storm, and it is allegedly also a remedy against the sting of scorpions and the bite of snakes. It is no great surprise that the shamrock was popularly adopted as a symbol for Ireland based on eighteenth-century legends about St Patrick; although the country's official emblem remains the harp, the shamrock remains the dominant symbol of all things Irish. It is commonly used as a badge for many Irish sports teams and enjoys broad cross-cultural acceptance, being used by Northern Irish teams and businesses as well as those in the Republic and even British military regiments such as the Irish guards.

The much rarer four-leaf clover is really an Irish symbol of luck. It is quite emphatically, however, *not* a shamrock and many a St Patrick's Day has supposedly been ruined by careless bakers and florists not understanding the difference. Finding a four-leaf clover, preferably accidentally, and then wearing it, brings the finder luck thanks to its extra leaf, alongside the faith, hope and love ascribed to the other three leaves. By other definitions the four leaves each represent a different lucky trait: respect, wealth, love and longevity.

The four-leaf clover's emergence as a symbolic myth

is likely to be derived from a mixture of threads of Irish folklore. From a spiritual perspective, it may represent the same divine trinity as that prescribed by St Patrick, but with the fourth leaf symbolizing man or humanity. The presence of this fourth leaf thus signifies redemption.

The four-leaf clover is rare, but this has not stopped particularly avid collectors amassing up to 160,000 of them. Furthermore, the luck dividend is not restricted: most collectors believe there is even more luck to be derived if you happen upon a five- or six-leaf clover, and so on. The claims for maximum number of leaves observed on a clover range from twenty-one to twenty-seven, though what exactly these extra leaves signify or by what factor the owner has more luck is not entirely clear. The odds of finding a five-leaf clover on a first attempt are one million to one, and the odds of finding anything with more than five leaves are minuscule, arguably indicating that, in the absence of any inordinately lucky horticulturalists, the whole legend is completely without statistical merit.

Shamrock and clover, though traditionally associated with Ireland, are more ubiquitous than one might assume. They can be found growing extensively in South America, at altitude in the tropics and Africa. The shamrock is featured on the passport stamp of the Caribbean island of

Montserrat as many of its citizens were originally of Irish origin. St Patrick's Day is celebrated there and it is the only country other than Ireland which celebrates the day as a national holiday.

The Battle to Become the 'Luckiest' Man in the World

According to the *Guinness Book of Records*, George Kaminski held the world record for the most 'found' four-leaf clovers until recently, amassing a collection of precisely 72,927 up to the point in 2005 when he had accrued enough 'luck' to be moved from the various high-security prisons he had been frequenting for the best part of his life into a minimum-security institution in Pennsylvania, which unfortunately had no access to clover grounds. Kaminski could only watch from the sidelines as his record was surpassed and eventually doubled – that's 160,000 clovers – by one resilient retiree, Edward Martin of Alaska.

Martin suggested that his good luck had helped keep him safe from aggressive grizzly bears and uppity wild moose while he searched their natural grazing grounds. Kaminski, meanwhile, suggested in a local newspaper interview, conducted via his parole officer and without a trace of irony, that Martin's luck had been founded on the fact that he had 'the entire world to look at' and not just the environs of various American penal institutions. Kaminski may yet come to the conclusion in quieter moments of self-reflection that he was overdrawn at the luck bank when he chose to take up kidnapping, abduction and extortion as a career path.

The Skull and Crossbones

The image of the skull and crossbones is immediately recognizable to most school children as the 'Jolly Roger', the universal sign of the pirate. The familiar image of a leering human skull above two crossed bones evokes a sense of savagery and danger while simultaneously representing the notion of honour amongst thieves: pirates, despite being known for devil-may-care anarchy, nonetheless adhered to a strict code of conduct. The 'pirate code' is thought to have been devised by a Portuguese buccaneer, Bartolomeu Português, a real-life 'Pirate of the Caribbean', who terrorized Spanish naval ships in the 1660s. Português instigated a series of 'articles of agreement' to govern the conduct of his crew, who in turn were required to swear an oath of allegiance on a human skull. Indeed, the principal purpose of the Jolly Roger, and of its all-red French predecessor the *Joli Rouge*

('Pretty Red'), from which the name is thought to derive, was to forewarn ships that they were about to be attacked – a level of customer service that seems at odds with the pirates' fearsome reputation.

The skull and crossbones symbol often adorns entrances to burial grounds in Latin America, such as this example from La Recoleta Cemetery in Buenos Aires, to protect the souls of the deceased from evil spirits and grave robbers

The symbol of the skull and crossbones, however, predates the advent of naval piracy by several centuries. In Hispanic cultures, the skull and crossbones symbol was historically displayed above the entrances to burial grounds to ward off evil spirits as well as grave robbers. Going further back still, it featured in some of the livery of the Poor Fellow-Soldiers of Christ and of the Temple of Solomon, more commonly known as the Knights Templar, a Christian military order active during the Crusades of the twelfth and thirteenth centuries. The order of the Knights Templar was disbanded by Pope Clement V in 1312, largely due to the fact that the order had become too powerful, amassing considerable wealth through the establishment of stringent and shrewd trade routes, banking and other business interests allied to their considerable military prowess. Modern-day freemasonry has an established historical relationship with the Knights Templar, borne out by the incorporation of Templar rituals and symbols into Masonic practices; the 'tracing board', an elaborately decorated piece of cloth or wooden board that features prominently in Masonic temples, includes images of the skull and crossbones.

Nowadays, inspired by its use in Spanish cemeteries, the skull and crossbones is most prominent as the international symbol for poison or toxic substances, a practice that began in New York State in 1829 and gradually spread around the world, as well as indicating potentially fatal hazards in public places.

The *Totenkopf* and German Military Insignias

The skull and crossbones has been used as a military insignia in many countries over recent centuries, but perhaps its most notable use was in Germany. The *Totenkopf* (literally 'Skull'), as the symbol is traditionally known, was first adopted by the Prussian army cavalry divisions under Frederick the Great in the eighteenth century and soon became a mainstay of the full Hussar uniform, with the image emblazoned on tunics and as a badge on the front of the distinctive *kucsma* ('busby') fur hats.

The symbol fell into relative disuse after the First World War, but in the 1930s leading Nazi Julius Schreck revived it as the emblem of the *Stabswache*, Hitler's personal regiment of bodyguards. It was subsequently adopted during the Second World War by various Waffen-SS Panzer divisions and squadrons of the Luftwaffe. At the behest of Heinrich Himmler the symbol was also forged on specially created silver rings that were presented as unofficial military awards to SS members after three years' service. To this day they are highly sought-after by collectors of ethically dubious memorabilia, often changing hands for considerable sums of money.

The Peace Symbol

Few iconic symbols of the latter half of the twentieth century can claim to have achieved global recognition on the scale of the peace symbol. Originally designed as an emblem of the fledgling Campaign for Nuclear Disarmament (CND) in Britain in the 1950s, the peace sign has become the universal indicator for anti-war movements.

The peace sign has been adopted at protests the world over; here a wall of peace signs forms a colourful part of the protests at Gezi Park, Istanbul, in June 2013

The peace symbol first appeared on banners and placards carried by protesters on the famous Aldermaston Peace March in April 1958. The march comprised several thousand anti-nuclear activists covering the fifty-two miles from Trafalgar Square – one of the most famous military memorials in Britain – to the Atomic Weapons Research Establishment that had been set up outside the village of Aldermaston in rural Berkshire eight years earlier. The protest was organized by a group of pacifists operating under the name of the Direct Action Committee (DAC), led by Hugh Brock, the editor of the anti-war publication *Peace News*. Brock enlisted the help of graphic artist and textile designer Gerald Holtom to produce a distinctive symbol to spearhead their protest, and Holtom devised a simple design that could easily be replicated on various fabrics and materials.

Holtom had originally wanted to use a Christian cross inside a circle as his design but came up against considerable opposition from members both of the church whom he approached for advice and supporters of the cause who felt it would confuse the message.

The symbol itself combines two basic meanings. In essence it is a drawing of a stick-like person with their arms lowered in a gesture of surrender or defeat. In a letter to Hugh Brock, Holtom wrote of his sign:

> I was in despair. Deep despair. I drew myself: the representative of an individual in despair, with hands palm outstretched outwards and downwards in the manner of Goya's peasant before the firing squad. I formalized the drawing into a line and put a circle round it.

The painting he is referring to is *The Shootings of the Third of May* by Francisco de Goya, although Holtom – a graduate of the Royal College of Art – misremembers Goya's classic anti-war image in which a condemned man has his arms raised aloft, almost in a gesture of incredulity and defiance.

Holtom's second interpretation of his design is that the downward-pointing arms of the figure combine the semaphore signals for N and D, representing 'Nuclear Disarmament'.

With the help of his wife and two daughters, Holtom produced 500 copies of his 'crow's foot within a circle' and affixed them to mock lollipop sticks of the sort commonly used by school crossing patrol officers near children's schools in the UK; he liked the association with protecting future generations from harm. The organizers of the march had originally anticipated that their protest would attract a hundred or so committed activists, but in the event over 10,000 people assembled at Trafalgar Square to show their support and join the walk to Aldermaston.

Due to the worldwide publicity the Aldermaston march attracted, Holtom's design was quickly adopted by CND as its official symbol and rapidly spread to peace movements in other countries. The uncomplicated elegance of the symbol made it extremely user-friendly and easy to draw or daub on walls. In the United States, it was readily adopted by anti-Vietnam War protesters and became a totem of counterculture groups of the late 1960s and 1970s. For the hippies of Haight-Ashbury in San Francisco the peace sign represented the war planes that bombed Hiroshima and Nagasaki and the B-52s blanket-bombing Vietnam. As a result, the symbol attracted a lot of derision from supporters of the war, with right-wing fundamentalists claiming the symbol had occultist roots or indicated Communist sympathies (see The Sign of Satan?, below).

But despite attempts to discredit the image and its meaning, Gerald Holtom's peace sign remains an enduring symbol of collective dissent against all forms of warfare and oppression.

The Sign of Satan?

The most concerted attempt to discredit the growing influence of the peace symbol centred round a bumper-sticker campaign in the United States in the early 1970s, during the final years of the Vietnam War. The growing anti-war movement had adopted the peace symbol as its motif, displaying it on placards and banners at mass rallies and spray-painting the image on VW Camper vans at music festivals. The ubiquity of the image was an obvious cause of concern for the pro-war lobby, in particular the ultra-conservative pressure group, the John Birch Society.

The John Birch Society had been formed in 1958 at the height of Cold War tensions and was an organization fervently driven by anti-Communist paranoia and far-right Christian fundamentalism. Among their more colourful Communist conspiracy theories was the belief that the civil rights movement of the 1960s was a Soviet propaganda campaign and that the fluoridization of water was a Communist plot to poison America. The latter theory was famously ridiculed by Stanley Kubrick in his 1964 film *Dr Strangelove*.

In the June 1970 edition of *American Opinion*, the journal of the John Birch Society, an article appeared under the title 'Peace Symbols: The Truth About Those Strange Designs', which set out an argument linking the peace symbol to

Satanism. The sign bears a passing resemblance to archaic pagan symbols such as 'the witch's foot' (also known as 'the crow's foot') and the inverted cross adopted by occultist sects. The inverted cross is thought to have its origins in the persecution of Christians under the Emperor Nero. The early Christian scholar Origen of Alexandria (AD 185–254) cites that St Peter was executed during Nero's purges and specifically requested to be crucified upside down, as he was not worthy of a death akin to Christ's. Occult groups have often used the upside-down cross as an emblem of their opposition to Christianity, though conversely Peter's request is generally seen as a sign of his Christian humility. The *American Opinion* article seized upon the coincidental similarity between the peace sign and an inverted cross and claimed, somewhat spuriously, that the icon of the peace movement was evidence of an evil and godless Communist plot to corrupt Christian values in the youth of America:

In America, as thousands of radicalized youths parade that same symbol, the heretics of The Christian have all but adopted the 'sign of the anti-Christ' as their own. And you can be absolutely certain that the Communists planned it that way.

In the months following the publication of the article, a billboard and bumper-sticker campaign sprang up, depicting the peace sign turned on its side to resemble a bomber plane, with the slogan 'The Footprint of the American Chicken'. The bumper stickers were thought to have been produced by the John Birch Society, which had an estimated 100,000 members at the time. Quite how they linked cowardice with Satanism and Communist propaganda is unclear but the Society was notoriously inconsistent in its rhetoric, having originally opposed the Vietnam War on the grounds that it was ... a Communist conspiracy.

The Olympic Rings

The modern Olympic Games, the brainchild of French aristocrat and intellectual Baron Pierre de Coubertin, made their debut in Athens in 1896. The dream that inspired de Coubertin to revive this ancient sporting spectacle was for the nations of the world to be brought together in a spirit of competition, which he hoped would encourage greater understanding of different cultures as well as promoting peace and unity.

But it was not until the fifth Olympiad, in Stockholm in 1912, that this vision was realized, for it was at these Games that all five inhabited continents were represented for the first time, thanks to the participation of Japan. Following a successful month of sport, in which women were permitted to take part in swimming and diving events for the first time and electronic timing was introduced to athletics, de Coubertin sent a positive report to the members of the

International Olympic Committee. He also sent them a design he had come up with for an Olympic logo: five interlocking coloured rings, to symbolize the five continents. The IOC approved the emblem and it was duly adopted as the official Olympic flag.

The Olympic rings were designed to unite all the flags of the competing nations. This monument to the spirit of the Games is a permanent fixture outside Montreal's Olympic Stadium

Contrary to popular belief, the logo's five colours do not correspond to particular continents; instead, when shown against a white background, they incorporate all the colours of the flags of the original competing nations.

Ironically, the 1916 Olympic Games, at which de Coubertin's symbol of international unity was due to make its glorious first appearance, were cancelled on account of the First World War. The Olympic flag did, however, fly at Antwerp in 1920, albeit this time with the notable absence of four of the founding nations – Germany, Austria, Bulgaria and Hungary – who were banned after objections by the Allied Nations. Future Olympic Games were also to witness their own political controversies but the five-ringed logo remains to this day the best-known sporting emblem in the world, serving as a defiant reminder – despite conflict, despite controversy – of the spirit of unity and togetherness its designer wished it to reflect.

Olympic Pictograms

As ever more nations joined the Olympic movement and participated in the Games, the scale of the logistics began to pose new obstacles for organizers. The most obvious problem centred on the language barriers inevitably created by gathering together most of the countries of the world. It was a problem not just of communication between individuals but also of communication about the events; any given sport might have dozens of different names in a variety of spellings and scripts. The ingenious answer was to develop a visual language that everyone could understand.

The now-familiar pictograms representing the Olympic sporting events seem as much a part of the symbolism of the Games as the five rings and the flaming torch. They were initially rolled out for London 1948 but much of the credit for our modern-day Olympic pictograms lies with the graphic designers behind the scenes at Tokyo 1964.

The organizers of the 1964 Games were faced

with a particularly tricky hurdle – pardon the pun – as they prepared to stage a global event for the first time, because traditional Japanese visual language and iconography were deemed too difficult to transpose into other languages and cultures, particularly as Japan had not adopted worldwide initiatives such as the 1949 Geneva Protocol on Road Signs and Signals. In an attempt to surmount the problem, a group of graphic designers led by Masaru Katsumi was set the task of creating a set of easily recognizable signs that could be universally understood.

Masaru and his team took inspiration from the pioneering work of Otto Neurath and Gerd Arntz at the Social and Economic Museum of Vienna. Neurath, a noted political scientist and philosopher, along with a team of visual artists, had developed a form of picture language called Isotype (International System Of TYpographic Picture Education) in the late 1920s and early 1930s. The principle behind Isotype was the creation of a visual language that could reflect social, technological, biological and historical information and connections in pictorial form. Gerd Arntz was a woodcut artist and illustrator who was one of the leading designers of Isotype, and his pared-down, geometric pictograms have had a lasting influence on the development of graphic design. The Japanese designers applied Arntz's pictographic principles to their designs for Tokyo 1964 and came up with a concise and consistent design framework that not only showcased modern, accessible Japan but also gave future Olympic organizers a benchmark of quality and innovation.

For the 1968 Mexico City Olympics the pictograms were further developed by American designer Lance Wyman, who took on board the basic pictographic system created by Masaru and his team and added Mexican folk-art elements and splashes of contemporary 1960s pop-art.

'A major difference between Katsumi's icons and ours,' he later recalled in an interview with *Smithsonian* magazine, 'is that the Tokyo sport icons were bold stick figures that incorporated the entire human figure. Our sport icons focused on an expressive detail, a part of the athlete's body or a piece of equipment, creating images similar to glyphs found in Mexican pre-Hispanic cultures. We relied heavily on the sport icons as communicators that could cross cultural and language barriers.'

Lance Wyman's pictograms and logos for the Mexico games are considered a masterpiece of modern graphic design and they paved the way for future graphic artists to develop pictographic images that reflected the history and culture of the host cities: Otl Aicher's icons for the Munich Games in 1972 were drawn on a specially created mathematical grid of horizontal and diagonal lines, a symbol of German geometric efficiency and modernism, while those used at Sydney 2000 incorporate the fluidity and colours of Aboriginal folk art into their design portfolio.

The Smiley

The journey of the yellow smiley face, from public relations initiative to the multi-faceted emoticon of modern communications, is a narrative that encompasses big business, popular culture, anti-establishment sentiment from the 1960s to the 1990s and a series of bitter copyright disputes.

One version of the story of 'the smiley' cites its origins in the city of Worcester, Massachusetts, New England's second most populous city, whose only previous claim to fame was as the birthplace of the adjustable monkey wrench and Shredded Wheat breakfast cereal. In 1963, Harvey Ball, a freelance advertising creative, received a commission to design a logo for the Worcester Mutual Insurance Company. Ball's employers were concerned that a recent merger with a rival insurance company was having a negative effect on staff morale and this was rubbing off on the company's customers. Legend has it that Ball grabbed a black felt-tip pen and drew a simple smiling face on a sheet of yellow paper to illustrate the new 'service with a smile' company ethos. Everyone loved it.

Worcester Mutual initially produced 1,000 button badges for employees to wear and to distribute to clients but the campaign proved so successful that they soon had to order a further 10,000 badges. Sadly the company did not recognize any commercial possibilities in the new logo and did not patent it. Ball himself is reputed to have received a one-off fee of $45 for his trouble, a sum that he later claimed he was more than happy with at the time.

The iconic smiley face, shown here on a 1999 United States postage stamp, has been the subject of great copyright debate since its appearance in 1963

As the distinctive yellow face was not copyrighted but had clearly struck a chord with the public, it was inevitable that somebody would pick up on the business potential of the smiley. Philadelphia-based brothers Bernard and Murray Spain owned a small retail company comprising several gift shops that sold novelties such as key rings, car bumper stickers and T-shirts. In the early 1970s the brothers started producing button badges, largely hoping to tap into the anti-Vietnam War peace movement, but instead stumbled upon a lucrative commercial proposition. As their badges began selling in extraordinary numbers, the Spains copyrighted the image along with the slogan 'Have a Happy Day' and branched out into a whole range of smiley-related merchandise. By 1973, the brothers' cottage industry in quaint novelty products had become a multi-million-dollar corporation with the smiley appearing on everything from lunchboxes to boxer shorts.

As the symbol developed into the ubiquitous icon of post-Vietnam America, the first copyright rumblings began to be heard. In France, a journalist and editor named Franklin Loufrani had adopted the smiley as an icon directing readers of the *France Soir* newspaper to the 'feel-good' stories in each issue. Loufrani always claimed that the image was in the public domain long before Harvey Ball is purported to have created it, citing its appearance in the 1948 Ingmar Bergman film *Port of Call* and its use as a promotional image for the New York rock 'n' roll radio station WMCA in the late 1950s and early 1960s. One of Loufrani's more spurious claims for the smiley being in the public domain, however, concerns the discovery of a small carved smiling face in a Neolithic cave in Nîmes.

In 1988 Loufrani, along with his son Nicolas, trademarked the smiley and set up the Smiley Company, which now owns the licence for the image in over a hundred countries worldwide and controls the use of the icon for commercial purposes. The dispute over the origins of the design remains unresolved. Harvey Ball was certainly the first to apply the image to a button badge and his design fitted the brief he was given, but it seems likely he may have seen the image somewhere before. In 2005 the US retail giant Wal-Mart attempted to hijack the smiley bandwagon by copyrighting the image, only to become embroiled in a bitter and protracted legal dispute with the Smiley Company, which Wal-Mart was eventually forced to abandon.

The smiley image has had a long and varied association with popular culture (see The Smiley in Popular Culture, p. 119) but in the twenty-first century it is most prevalent in the use of emoticons. The first font-based emoticon,

:-), is attributed to Scott Fahlman, a computer scientist at Carnegie Mellon University in Pennsylvania. In 1982, Fahlman was setting up a message board for his students and proposed that the sideways smile should be used to mark up light-hearted postings. As use of the internet spread rapidly, the sideways smile became a standard symbol in emails, chat rooms and on bulletin boards, and many other variations were developed to express more complex emotions. By 1997 Nicolas Loufrani was experimenting with animated smiley faces and compiled an online emoticon dictionary, which contains over 2,000 entries.

The growth of mobile phones and other handheld devices has contributed to the popularity of smiley emoticons, which now provide shorthand symbols for a whole gamut of human expressions and emotions. In less than fifty years the smiley symbol has developed from a simple public relations stunt to a visual language in its own right.

The Smiley in Popular Culture

The Spain brothers initially adopted the smiley logo to cash in on the Woodstock era of flower power and anti-war demonstrations, as a result of which the smiley has long had an association with anti-establishment sentiment.

In 1979, collage artists Bob Last and Bruce Slesinger used smileys in place of swastikas for the cover of punk band Dead Kennedys' record *California Über Alles*. The cover depicted Governor of California Jerry Brown addressing a right-wing political rally with smileys drawn on the Nazi flags behind the podium.

In the UK in 1988, the so-called 'second summer of love', the smiley became the emblem of the acid house craze. DJ Danny Rampling used the logo on flyers for his London clubnight, Shoom, and within months the smiley had become the ubiquitous symbol of a new youth movement, appearing on T-shirts and record covers. Grunge band Nirvana adapted the smiley logo in the early 1990s, giving the distinctive yellow face crossed eyes and a dribbling mouth on their 'Corporate Rock Whore' merchandising.

The smiley has also featured in comic books, most notably Alan Moore's seminal graphic novel *Watchmen* (1987), in which a blood-stained version appeared as a recurring theme, although in the 1970s it had adorned the cover of *Mad* magazine and also taken the form of a sinister masked gangster named Boss Smiley in the DC comic *Prez*.

Robert Zemeckis's 1994 film *Forrest Gump* contains a jokey reference to the creation of the smiley icon. In one scene the eponymous character has his face splattered in mud and a wellwisher hands him a yellow T-shirt with which to clean himself. When Forrest hands back the shirt the imprint of his face has accidentally created the smiley logo.

PART THREE

SYMBOLS OF VALUE, OWNERSHIP AND EXCHANGE

'When a ruling class measures its fortunes, not by the acre of land or the ingot of gold, but by the number of figures corresponding ideally to a certain number of exchange operations, it thereby condemns itself to setting a certain kind of humbug at the centre of its experience and its universe. A society founded on signs is, in its essence, an artificial society in which man's carnal truth is handled as something artificial.'

Albert Camus

The answer to the question of which of the ancient civilizations 'invented' money is hotly debated by historians. The existence of early Greek and Roman coins shows that monetary systems existed at least as early as the seventh century BC, although a culture of bartering goods was undoubtedly prevalent in both societies and cultures much earlier – and no doubt was still commonly used for transactions long after the creation of objects with ascribed economic value.

Early coins were minted in the precious metals of gold and silver, two substances that have held a timeless fascination and have themselves retained symbolic as well as economic importance in human societies. If, as is often suggested, the first functioning fiscal system was devised by the Ancient Greeks, it also follows that they were the first society to attempt to verify the ownership of ideas by issuing patents and copyrights. Perhaps Albert Camus is correct in his assertion that the creation of a society based on signs and symbols of value, ownership and exchange replaced more natural egalitarian principles of solidarity. The relatively obscure story of the use of fire insurance marks, also revealed in this chapter, is conceivably a case in point, in that the dilemma of whether or not to enter a burning building was determined not by assessing the potential risk or danger, but rather by the type of symbol placed above the door ...

Currency Symbols

The Pound

If you've ever thought the symbol denoting the British pound sterling looks rather like a fancy L with a line through it, you were quite right: that's exactly what it is.

The pound's origins date back to the late eighth century, when King Offa of Mercia introduced a currency system based on that established in mainland Europe by his contemporary, Emperor Charlemagne. Under Offa's new system, as in Charlemagne's, 240 silver pennies weighed one pound, which in the Latin of Charlemagne's empire was known as one *libra* – from which we also get the lb used to denote pounds of weight. When the pound itself became a unit of currency, the L of *libra* was adopted as its symbol. The one or two bars through the pound sign clarify that the L is being used as a symbol, as indeed they do in the Y of the Japanese yen (¥).

This Scottish pound note from 1967 shows the pound sign's origins as a capital L, for *libra*

The Euro

The symbol for the euro, one of the world's newest and largest currencies, looks very straightforward and indeed quite uninteresting, yet its design was shrouded in the kind of mystery usually reserved for the election of a new pope. An initial thirty designs were whittled down to ten, and then two, with the final choice made by the European Commission, which refused to release details of the also-ran designs.

The logo is broadly based on the symbol for the notional European Currency Unit that preceded it, which was simply an intertwined C and E (₠), although the European Commission claimed more whimsical inspiration when it unveiled the euro in 1996: 'Inspiration for the € symbol came from the Greek epsilon (Є) – a reference to the cradle of European civilization – and the first letter of the word Europe, crossed by two parallel lines to "certify" the stability of the euro.'

Given the currency's woes over the past few years, the European Commission may want to rethink those two parallel lines.

The Dollar

The word 'dollar' dates back to sixteenth-century silver coins minted in the town of Joachimsthal in what is now the Czech Republic. The coins were originally known as *Joachimsthaler*, or *thaler* for short, and as the word gradually spread into other European languages the 'thaler' became the 'taler' and eventually the 'dollar'. Evidence of the use of the word 'dollar' to denote pieces of silver can be found in Shakespeare, most notably in *Macbeth* (Ross: 'Nor would we deign [the Norwegian king] burial of his men Till he disbursed ... Ten thousand dollars to our general use' – Act

I, scene ii) – although this was probably an unintentional anachronism on the part of the Bard as *Macbeth* is set several centuries before thalers or dollars came into existence. The symbol for the dollar arrived much later, although its origins remain unclear and have given rise to various different theories.

One popular (albeit tenuous) theory, particularly among American patriots, is that the dollar sign with two vertical strokes is derived from the initials of the United States. If a capital U is superimposed on a capital S, with the lower part of the U dissolved into the bottom curve of the S, the resulting symbol is a two-stroke dollar sign. There is, however, some dispute as to the legitimacy of this theory, although it is championed by a character in the novel *Atlas Shrugged* (1957) by Republican-leaning American writer Ayn Rand.

The more commonly received wisdom on the origins of the dollar symbol is that it is derived from the Spanish peso, which travelled to the New World with the conquistadors. The original abbreviation of 'peso' was a capital P in the singular, and P with a raised lower-case *s* in the plural: P[s]. Over time this was simplified to just the upward stroke of the P with the *s* drawn over it, which was ultimately adopted as the single-stroke dollar sign.

Although this explanation is the most widely accepted, its main failing is that it doesn't really account for the existence of two-stroke dollar symbols. One theory that does account for this anomaly is that the Spanish peso – or 'piece of eight' coin of pirate folklore – was engraved with a representation of the two Pillars of Hercules, which later inspired the two-stroke symbol. That said, these same coins were minted at the Spanish colonial mint in Potosí, Bolivia, and bore the letters PTSI, superimposed on top of each other, as a hallmark of origin; the resultant effect was that the combined characters resembled the modern single-stroke dollar symbol.

A variation of the peso-related theory concerns the colloquial term 'piece of eight', which came about because a peso was equivalent in value to eight smaller silver coins known as reals. The peso was represented as P8, or the number 8 enclosed within two downward strokes, and over time it became fashionable simply to strike through the figure 8 with the vertical lines.

for Esclavo

One of the more sinister theories concerning the origin of the dollar symbol is that it may be derived from the Spanish words for 'slave' and 'nail'. The iron shackles used to restrict slaves for transportation or imprisonment were locked by nails that had been passed through the rings of the chains and then bent into a loop. The Spanish word for 'slave' is *esclavo* and 'nail' is the very similar *clavo*. The theory is that the $ is a visual abbreviation of 'S-clavo' – *S* for 'slave' or *esclavo*, with the downward stroke representing the nail used to enchain the prisoners – and that it was used in slave traders' accounting to denote the number of slaves in their possession. Although a plausible and grimly interesting theory, there is no known evidence of this practice in slave trading records.

Maths
Symbols

Pi

We're all familiar with the symbols used in mathematics to denote relative value, but very few people know what they actually mean.

Pi, which represents the ratio of a circle's circumference to its diameter and is a famously never-ending, non-repeating number beginning 3.14, is symbolized by π, a Greek letter equivalent to p. But what has the letter p to do with anything? The first use of π in the context of circumference seems to have been in a 1706 book by Welsh mathematician William Jones, who employed it as an abbreviation of 'periphery' – although William Oughtred had used it a generation earlier, also to mean 'periphery', in a different mathematical context. Other mathematicians continued to use the non-Greek p, or simply to write out the full word, until 1748, when the highly influential Leonhard Euler decreed that π should become standardized. 'For the sake of brevity we will write this number as π,' he wrote in *Introductio in analysin infinitorum*. 'Thus π is equal to half the circumference of a circle of radius 1.'

Per Cent

The percentage sign looks at first as if it represents two quantities of equal value – which is ironic, since it actually indicates the extent to which one quantity is smaller than another. So why the two zeros (or dots, as they tend to appear when handwritten)? Until the fourteenth century it was customary for traders, accountants and indeed mathematicians to refer to a quantity *per cento*, 'for [every] one hundred' in Italian. To save time this was often written 'per 100' or 'p 100' with a line through the stem of the p to indicate an abbreviation. Then, in the early fifteenth century, there is evidence of people using the abbreviation pc beside a horizontal line and the superscript 'o' of *cento*, so that it looked more like this: pc—°. Over the next two centuries the abbreviation disappeared and the 'o' was joined by another, beneath the line. And that's all there is to it.

The Octothorpe

It is not uncommon for the meaning of common symbols to evolve within a number of different contexts, but few of them have had such a variety of usages as #. The historical origins of the symbol are both obscure and contradictory, further clouded by confusion concerning its 'official' name. There are a variety of terms used to denote it, the most common being 'pound sign', 'number sign', 'libra', 'octothorpe' and 'hash sign' or – thanks largely to Twitter – 'hashtag', in addition to multiple variations relating to computer programming.

Prior to rapid advances in telecommunications and computer technology, the sign was generally used to denote quantities or units of weight (hence 'pound'): 3# of apples, 2# of tomatoes. In US newspapers the results of horse races were often printed using the # symbol to denote the order of running: #1 Seabiscuit, #2 War Emblem, and so on. The *Oxford English Dictionary* ascribes the early use of the term 'pound sign' to typewriting manuals popular in the 1920s, although its origins remain unclear. One possible explanation is that it is a shorthand symbol for the more formal abbreviation for pound, 'lb'. This may account for the # symbol sometimes being called the 'libra', for which 'lb' is the standard abbreviation from Latin for the Roman unit of weight.

The decline of the usage of # to denote weight or numerical order coincided with the creation of the touch-tone telephone in the late 1960s. It was at this point that the symbol was renamed the octothorpe by a Bell Laboratories executive named Don Macpherson, who was charged with training clinic staff in Minnesota to use a new telephone exchange system that relied on innovative push-button commands including the 'number sign': #. Macpherson decided he needed a name for the symbol to include in his training sessions and came up with the name 'octothorpe' – 'octo', presumably, because the sign has eight points. The addition of 'thorpe' as a suffix is thought to be something of an in-joke by Macpherson, who was renowned at Bell Labs for his offbeat sense of humour. In his spare time, he was involved in a campaign to have the gold medals won by the American athlete James Francis 'Jim' Thorpe at the 1912 Olympics reinstated (See 'The Greatest

Athlete You've Never Heard Of', opposite).

As the term 'octothorpe' was subsequently written into Bell Labs' training manuals and other company documents, it eventually became the accepted official name for the symbol on telephone keypads. Developing technology saw it become a standard command function, not only for internal telephone networks but for automated answering systems used by commercial corporations for a myriad of purposes, ranging from telephone banking transactions to customer service complaints.

Developments in information technology have added additional uses to the # sign, notably in the UNIX operating system and in programming languages such as Perl and C++, where it performs an array of functions and commands. The rapid growth of the internet has added further dimensions to the sign that are far removed from its origin denoting weight or numbers. On Twitter and other social networking sites, for instance, the symbol is used both as part of a metadata tag, to group messages with a shared subject, and to herald a light-hearted comment or mood.

The Greatest Athlete You've Never Heard Of

Many top athletes have excelled in more than one sporting discipline but the extraordinary achievements of American Jim Thorpe remain beyond all comparison.

James Francis Thorpe was born on Indian Territory in Oklahoma in 1888 and brought up in a Sac and Fox Native American tribe. His early life was blighted by tragedy, with the sudden deaths of his mother and twin brother from pneumonia, and he dropped out of school and drifted for a number of years, working as a farm hand before attending the Carlisle Indian Industrial School. It was here that Thorpe's extraordinary athletic ability came to the attention of legendary sports coach Pop Warner.

Thorpe initially excelled at track and field events before persuading Warner to let him play American football, too. Thorpe's immense strength and speed made him a phenomenal running back, and it was largely thanks to him that Carlisle beat

Harvard University 18–15 to win the 1912 National College Championships, a game in which Thorpe scored all of his team's points.

Warner encouraged Thorpe to try out for the US Olympic team, and after storming the trials with his all-round abilities he was entered for both the pentathlon and decathlon at the 1912 Olympics in Stockholm. Thorpe went on to become the star of the games, winning gold medals in both multidisciplinary events and narrowly missing out on medals in the long jump and high jump. When King Gustav V of Sweden was presenting medals at the closing ceremony, he reportedly told Thorpe he was 'the greatest athlete in the world'.

Despite returning to America a national hero, Thorpe's obvious athletic superiority attracted the attention of right-wing elements in the media who resented his Native American background. In the year following the Olympics, a series of newspaper articles attacked him on the grounds that he had violated the 'amateurs only' Olympic code. Thorpe had briefly played Minor League baseball, largely as a means of making a small amount of money during the summer holidays while at college, and had been unaware that he was contravening any regulations. Nonetheless, on the instruction of the American Athletics Union, the International Olympic Committee stripped him of his medals.

Thorpe went on to have a successful career as a professional sportsman, playing Major League baseball with the New York Giants and the Boston Braves, and American football for the Cleveland Indians. He even found time to turn out for an all-Indian basketball team in semi-professional exhibition games.

Thorpe died in 1953 at the age of sixty-four, but interest in his career and in particular his harsh treatment by the athletics authorities was revived in the early 1960s after President Eisenhower – who'd played college football against Thorpe – praised him in a speech as 'America's greatest ever athlete'. This led to a determined campaign to have the 1912 Olympic gold medals reinstated, a campaign during which Bell Labs' executive

Don Macpherson immortalized the great athlete in the new name he bestowed upon the humble hashtag. Finally, in 1983, thirty years after Thorpe's death, the IOC overruled its original decision and presented two replica medals to Thorpe's children at a special ceremony.

Symbols of Ownership

Copyright

The universal copyright sign was first introduced by the United States Congress via the Copyright Act of 1909. The previous provision for copyrighting material dated back to 1790 and was considered inadequate in dealing with modern printing and reproduction methods. President Theodore Roosevelt had proposed an overhaul of the copyright laws in a speech to Congress in 1905, declaring the previous laws 'difficult for the courts to interpret and impossible for the Copyright Office to administer'. The law was drafted under the direction of the Librarian of Congress, Herbert Putnam, who undertook consultations with publishers and artists' organizations.

One stumbling block in the details of the act proved to be the requirement for works of art to display a notice stating that copyright had been obtained and was therefore protected by federal law. Published printed material had long contained either the word 'copyrighted' or the abbreviation 'copr' but works of fine art were now thought to be in need of protection. Artists' groups objected to the idea that paintings needed to have 'copyright' written beneath the artist's signature and so a compromise was drawn up whereby a simple symbol of a C encased in a circle could be displayed instead. Initially only works of fine art such as paintings and illustrations were allowed to use it but further amendments to the act allowed it to be used on printed materials as a universally recognized symbol.

Trademark

The use of trademarks or logos is thought to date from the Roman Empire; blacksmiths producing swords for the Roman armies often inscribed initials or symbols on the handles of weapons to identify their maker.

By the late medieval period European craftsmen producing goods in precious metals were required by law to mark their wares with a hallmark to denote that the raw material used was of the correct level of purity. The word 'hallmark' dates from a charter granted in 1327 by King Edward III to a guild of metalworkers who became known as the Worshipful Company of Goldsmiths, based in Goldsmiths' Hall in London. The hallmark to confirm that an article produced by the guild met with the sterling silver standard of 92.5 per cent purity was the symbol of a leopard's head, a motif thought to have been inspired by the royal arms. Other guilds sprang up across the country, and then across continental Europe, each adopting a distinctive symbol or emblem to denote the origin of the goods produced and the official stamp of the quality of master craftsmen.

The advent of mass-production techniques and the developments of the Industrial Revolution in the eighteenth and nineteenth centuries led to other craftsmen and traders looking at ways to make their products distinctive, of renowned origin and of visible quality. The use of trademarks by large and ever more global companies inevitably led to concerns about the counterfeiting of goods and products. In the United Kingdom, legislation was passed in 1862 to protect against the fraudulent use of 'merchandise marks' and this was further extended by the Trademarks Act of 1875, which allowed companies to register their trademarks with the Patents Office.

As a general rule, registered trademarks are denoted by the ® symbol while unregistered ones bear the mark ™.

Gold and Silver in Symbology

Gold's relative rarity and almost universally ascribed value means that it has generally been used to convey positive symbolic meaning. We reward our athletes and high achievers with gold medals that not only have actual value but also imbue a sense of greatness. Indeed, even in very superficial contexts the prefix 'gold' implies superiority. Take, for example, 'Golden Balls' – supposedly Victoria Beckham's nickname for her husband David. Thus we treat others by the golden rule, give gold cards to valued customers or ascribe quasi-religious meaning to natural constants such as the golden ratio.

As a colour, gold is associated with the sun, God in his many forms and all notions of royalty. A symbol, therefore, of success, happiness, friends and rejoicing, gold is perhaps the only colour that has no negative connotations, save for an association with vulgarity – 'bling' – and needless excess. King Midas had a golden touch that we still invoke today to describe someone with the 'knack' – although it is often used with a degree of envy, as if to imply good, if not wholly deserved, fortune. When retelling the myth of King Midas we conveniently overlook the fact that his lucky streak only lasted until he became hungry or embraced one of his children, depending on which version you read. He was permitted to wash his power away in the River Pactolus, thus explaining its richness in gold, although he still did not get away scot-free, suffering in later life the indignity of having his ears turned into those of an ass, after a disagreement with the god Apollo regarding his musical ability. Likewise the myth of Jason, of Argonauts fame, who did indeed capture the treasured Golden Fleece but then ended his days as a pitiful drunk and died when the rotting stern of the *Argo* fell on him while he was sleeping off a drinking binge.

The periodic symbol for gold is Au, although this is less of a symbol and more a literal description, according to chemical convention, using its Latin name: *aurum. Aurum* in turn means either 'shining down' or 'shining dawn', an association with the sun. The symbolic connection between the sun and gold is prevalent in many ancient civilizations, most notably the great Inca Empire that flourished in South America during the fifteenth and early sixteenth centuries. The Incas worshipped the sun, and the abundance of gold, which they mined extensively, allied with their considerable skills in metalwork, enabled them to decorate their palaces and temples with precious metals. The shiny, reflective nature of gold entranced the Incas, whose whole spiritual belief system was based around the sun and the moon; for them, gold was the sweat of the sun, while silver (which they also mined) was the tears of the moon. Sadly, however, it was gold, the very thing they revered most, that brought about the demise of their empire and civilization when the Spanish conquistadors arrived in search of the riches of the New World.

Gold has been a status symbol for mankind since time immemorial, and features in the legend of Jason and the Argonauts, who risked life and limb to capture the Golden Fleece

Silver suffers in its eternal comparison and association with gold. It symbolizes many of the things that gold does, but just not quite to the same extent. In modern culture there is an element of 'second best' about silver, typified by the awarding of silver medals to second-placed athletes; many silver medals have allegedly ended up in various bins, rivers and skips around Olympic venues over the years, courtesy of disgruntled competitors for whom silver meant nothing but 'top loser'.

In folklore, silver often has connotations of poison and death, particularly in vampire mythology – silver crosses repel blood-sucking demons, silver bullets destroy werewolves, etc. – and it is in its macabre iteration that silver far outstrips gold in symbolic interest. As gold is associated with the sun, so silver has been linked with the moon – and therefore with the night, with mystery and magic. Although gold has its connotations of excess, the biblical parable of Judas taking his 'thirty pieces of silver' has entered modern parlance to describe someone who forsakes that which is apparently dearest to him for an immediate reward that proves insubstantial in the end, or who simply behaves treacherously through self-interest.

Elvis And Liberace:
Excess All Areas

Gold has long been associated with deities, royalty and rulers, many of whom legitimized their status through their symbolic appropriation of gold, so perhaps it is not surprising that Elvis Presley, the self-styled 'King' of rock 'n' roll, and his showman contemporary, Liberace, shared an unquenchable thirst for all things gilded and auriferous.

Of Elvis's many gold-related possessions, the most famous were his trademark gold suits. The first gold suit was designed by Nudie Cohn, a Hollywood tailor, in 1957. The material used was lamé, a fabric made by weaving together ribbons of fine, flexible cheap metal alloys. Elvis insisted on using strips of genuine gold leaf in the construction of his suit, at an estimated cost of $10,000 (around $100,000 today). Alongside his gold suits and extensive collection of rare and astronomically expensive watches – all in varying degrees of gold, of course – Elvis had a specially commissioned 1965 Cadillac Eldorado constructed containing numerous gold parts (steering wheel, bumpers, etc.) and hand-painted with over forty coats of gold leaf paint.

It seemed there was little left in the world made of gold that Elvis couldn't acquire by one means or another, but there was one small gold symbol he craved that couldn't be acquired with money alone. On 21 December 1970, he met President Richard Nixon at the White House. Three days earlier, Presley had sent a letter to Nixon stating his support and admiration for the president and (ironically) offering his help in the battle against drug culture and Communist indoctrination. He had requested the opportunity to serve his country as a 'Federal Agent at Large'. In truth, however, Presley's real motivation was to get his hands on the famous standard-issue Gold Star Badge given to agents of the United States.

Liberace, the other great American showman of the 1950s and 1960s, was no less excessive and flamboyant when it came to gold. Liberace's love of gold extended to pianos specially constructed with golden keys, a gold-plated Bradley GT sports car, numerous gold stage clothes and, most alarmingly of all, a gold-plated toilet with a seat encrusted with 18-carat gold coins.

Fire Insurance Marks

In the early hours of 2 September 1666, a fire broke out in a small London bakery owned by Thomas Farriner. The conflagration, fanned by strong winds, rapidly spread across the city, destroying over 13,000 houses and many significant public buildings, including the original St Paul's Cathedral. Although there were many contributing factors behind the disaster that became known as the Great Fire of London, such as tinder-dry wooden houses that were built virtually on top of each other and the failure of the relevant authorities to act swiftly enough to take measures to contain the fire, there were simply no organized groups trained to fight fires, and such water supplies and firefighting equipment as were available were totally inadequate to stop a fire of such magnitude from spreading.

A fire insurance mark indicating that this house in South London was covered by the Hand in Hand Insurance Society, established in 1696

In the aftermath of the catastrophe, various initiatives were put in place to help prevent such devastation from occurring again. Building regulations were drawn up to govern both the construction of buildings and the width of the streets between them, and systems designed to improve firefighting facilities and water supplies. One of the repercussions of the Great Fire was the number of disputes between landlords and tenants regarding who was liable for damage to properties, who should be compensated for their loss and who should pay for the rebuilding. Charles II set up a special Fire Court to deal with the various claims and counterclaims, and it sat for five whole years, from 1667 to 1672. One of the Court's most significant recommendations was that properties should be insured against fire damage.

By 1680 the first fire insurance company, the Fire Office, had been established in London. In contrast to modern insurance practice, owners didn't insure their property for a particular value against the likelihood of damage by fire, but rather they paid for an insurance policy that guaranteed that, in the event of a fire, all possible attempts would be made to save their property and belongings from destruction. In essence, the Fire Office was a private fire brigade available only to those willing to pay for the service.

The success of the Fire Office led to ever more fire insurance companies being set up, most notably the Friendly Society (1683) and the Hand in Hand (1696), each with its own affiliated fire brigade. Typically, a company brigade would employ between eight and thirty firefighters, mostly on an ad hoc basis, who were paid for each fire they attended, although brigade foremen were often paid a retaining salary.

As the number of fire insurance companies grew, it became necessary to distinguish which property was insured by which particular company. This led to the practice of placing 'fire marks' – copper or lead plaques – on the exteriors of buildings, often above the doorway, which were easily identifiable from the street. Each company had its own distinctive plaque comprising of the company insignia or emblem, a sort of coat of arms or crest, and a reference number relating to the type and scope of the policy the property owner had taken out.

It seemed a straightforward enough solution, but competition for business between the fire insurance companies soon led to confusion over the extent to which a brigade was duty-bound to fight fires in properties insured by rival companies. It was not uncommon, for example, for a brigade to be summoned to a fire at a certain property only to discover that it was insured by another company, and therefore to refuse to tackle the blaze through fear of not receiving remuneration. It was also an established practice for insurance companies to remove fire marks from properties where either the policy had lapsed or the owner was behind with insurance payments.

Gradually the number of fire insurance companies dwindled as several companies, in a spirit of cooperation, pooled the resources of their respective brigades, which culminated in the formation of the London Fire Brigade Establishment in 1833. By the mid-nineteenth century, however, the cost and logistics of running and maintaining a fire service had become too unwieldy for the insurance conglomerates and they lobbied parliament for the creation of a publicly funded fire service, a request that was granted in 1865.

Although the practice of placing fire marks on buildings more or less ceased, many can still be found on buildings in older areas of Britain, as well as in the United States and parts of Australia, where similar fire insurance schemes operated in the eighteenth and nineteenth centuries.

PART FOUR

Symbols of Protection, Direction and Survival

'Life is one big road with lots of signs,
so when you riding through the ruts,
don't you complicate your mind.'

Bob Marley, 'Wake Up and Live'

The most utilitarian use of signs is in the proliferation of symbols that direct and protect us, from road signs announcing locations and distances to international symbols warning of dangers and hazards. From an early age we learn the colours and shapes associated with these signs and how they point us towards what is permitted and away from what is forbidden or best avoided. People also rely on signs and codes for survival, which is why this chapter also looks at hoboglyphs, an all-but-lost symbolic language, and the development of sign languages for the deaf.

Road Traffic Signs

Traffic signs are part of everyday life. Made up of simple shapes and colours, they are etched in our minds to such a degree that we interpret and obey them almost subconsciously.

Route 66 and its iconic symbol have become entrenched in American culture, despite the highway having been replaced by the Interstate system during the 1980s

Today's signs evolved from Roman milestones, which literally were large columns set at mile intervals along busy highways. The information they provided varied from place to place across the empire, but might include names of and directions to the nearest towns or even the distance to Rome ('all roads lead to Rome', after all). The system was expanded during the Middle Ages to include new directions to new places, although many Roman milestones can still be seen today.

It was an increase in the use of the bicycle in the late nineteenth century that created the necessity for something other than basic direction and distance; the condition of the road and the steepness of any inclines became important factors to convey. The Touring Club Ciclistico Italiano was one of the key players in the late 1890s, advocating the standardization of road signs and producing its own highly detailed cycling maps. A number of international conferences around the turn of the century, notably the 1908 International Road Congress in Rome, established the basic principles of a unified set of traffic symbols, and by the 1950s most – though not all – countries had adopted the dozens of signs we are all familiar with today. The USA did not acquiesce until the 1960s and still employs the widest variety of shapes in its signage, with certain variations from state to state; arguably its most famous road sign, the shield indicating Route 66, refers to a 4,000-kilometre highway that has a fond place in popular culture despite having been replaced by the Interstate system in the 1980s.

Britain characteristically held out considerably longer than its European neighbours, until it could no longer deny that its plucky idiosyncrasy and plethora of chaotically inconsistent road signs might actually cost lives. The mess of different symbols, colours, shapes and typefaces across the country meant drivers really had to read the signs rather than understand them at a distance, which was particularly dangerous at a time when the government was investing heavily in an ambitious programme of motorway construction.

Something had to be done, and the graphic designers who devoted ten years to doing it, from 1957 to 1967, were Jock Kinneir and his student Margaret Calvert. They devised a rigorous signage system of carefully coordinated lettering, colours, shapes and symbols that was efficient and elegant, and one of the most ambitious information design projects ever undertaken in Britain. It remains a role model for modern road signage in other countries and is still in use today.

The codes adopted by Kinneir and Calvert conformed to the European protocol of using triangular signs to warn drivers, circles to issue commands, and rectangles to relay information. They used white lettering against a blue background for motorways, white lettering for place names and yellow for road numbers against a green background for primary roads, and black lettering against a white background for secondary routes. All type was in a curvaceous typeface called Transport, created specially by Kinneir and Calvert and designed with legibility in all weather conditions in mind. Their use of upper- and lower-case lettering distinguished the road signs from other adverts and notices drivers might come across en route.

One of Margaret Calvert's best-loved UK road signs, if only for the fact that it resembles not so much a 'man at work' as a 'man struggling with umbrella'

Where practical, and in keeping with European protocol, pictograms replaced typography, and Calvert drew most of these in the simple, friendly style of the Transport typeface. Many of them were inspired by her own life: the cow featured in the triangular sign warning of nearby farm animals, for instance, was based on Patience, a cow on her relatives' farm. One of her most famous signs – school children crossing the road – was adapted from an existing sign of a little boy leading a little girl by the hand; wanting 'to make it more inclusive because the comprehensive school system was starting up', Calvert swapped the roles so that a little girl – based on herself as a child – was leading a younger boy.

Perhaps the most iconic of Calvert's pictograms is the one indicating 'men at work', not so much because it's particularly helpful for approaching motorists but rather because it's one of her few bloopers, resembling – and fondly known as – 'man struggling with umbrella'.

The London Underground Map

There can be few civic transport systems in the world as iconic as the London Underground, particularly in terms of its distinctive use of signage and graphic design. The world-renowned image of the Underground map has inspired everything from fashion garments and modern art works to board games, wallpaper and shower curtains. The topographical structure of the map has also been adopted by many other rapid transport systems around the world, making the 'Tube map', as it is commonly known, truly a design classic.

When what is now known as the London Underground began as a loose network of underground railways built and managed by several different firms in the late nineteenth century, fierce competition between the companies meant there wasn't much impetus to provide a coherent map of the network as a whole. The early maps were geographically accurate maps of the city with the locations of each station marked on top. As the network grew, with more and more stations added to the respective lines, the maps became increasingly cluttered and confusing, particularly in central areas. With the dawn of electrification and the need to provide passengers with interchanges between lines, the separate companies gradually collaborated on practicalities from engineering to maps and ultimately merged as London Transport in 1933.

The new company needed an urgent solution to its chaotic geographical mapping and with some reluctance considered a topographical map designed by Harry Beck, an engineering draughtsman at the London Underground Signals Office. Beck had realized that showing the accurate geographical location of each station was superfluous information for most passengers, since they were travelling underground and just wanted to know they could get from A to B. He redrew the map using only straight lines of various colours running horizontally, vertically and at angles of forty-five degrees. The only geographical element was a rough approximation of the contours of the Thames, so that passengers knew if they were heading north or south of the river.

London Underground Map
Designed by Harry Beck

Harry Beck received scant financial reward for his revolutionary Tube map but his standing as a design genius has been recognized in recent years, such as on this 1999 'Design Classics' stamp

Beck submitted his design to Frank Pick, the chief executive of London Transport, but was initially met with considerable scepticism; Pick was concerned that the map gave no accurate measurement of the distances between stations. Pick grudgingly agreed to a trial print-run of the map, however, and to his surprise Beck was proved right: the new map was an instant hit with travellers, who snapped up all 700,000 copies.

As Harry Beck hadn't been officially commissioned to produce the map and had done so very much as a labour of love, he received scant financial reward for his revolutionary design, thought to be as little as ten guineas. Beck continued to amend and update his design up until the 1960s but fell foul of internal politics and quite possibly the jealousy of fellow employees. Further amendments and alterations were added by other officially commissioned designers as new stations and lines were built and older stations shut down, but the Tube map as it is today, in terms of structure and design, owes everything to the ingenuity of Harry Beck.

Possibly embarrassed by their treatment of Beck and their failure to acknowledge his contribution to the company, it was many years before London Transport authorities gave Harry Beck the recognition his endeavours deserved. Belated tribute was finally accorded in the early 1990s, two decades after Beck's death, when a gallery of the London Transport Museum was named after him and his original drawings and designs placed on permanent display.

Sign Languages

One of the common misconceptions about the sign language used by deaf people is that it is a universally intelligible system of common hand signals. In actuality there is no worldwide standard for sign language, despite attempts over the years to establish one. Sign languages developed independently of one another and vary from country to country, with certain similar gestures holding differing meanings from one system to the next.

The first recorded attempt to formalize a sign language for the deaf was by a Spanish priest in the early seventeenth century. Juan Pablo Bonet was employed as an attendant to a high-ranking Spanish nobleman, Juan Fernández de Velasco, the Duke of Frias, and became tutor to Luis, the duke's deaf and mute son. It was a period in which people with such disabilities were stigmatized and largely considered to be unteachable simpletons, but the enlightened priest attempted to overcome this obstacle by developing a system of hand signals and gestures corresponding to the alphabet as an aid to teaching Luis basic literacy – a legal requirement for the heirs of titled Spanish houses.

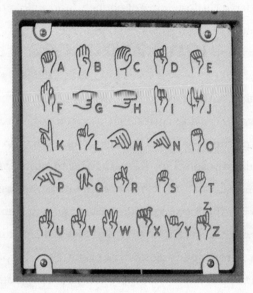

The development of sign language, shown here on a plaque in a school playground, revolutionized life for millions of deaf people around the world

Word of Bonet's system quickly spread and he was soon in demand to teach other deaf and mute offspring of the Spanish nobility. He refined his system and in 1620 published *Reducción de las letras y arte para enseñar a hablar a los mudos* (*Reduction of Letters and Art for Teaching Mute People to Speak*), a manual outline of his methods with illustrative engravings showing the different hand gestures and their corresponding letters of the alphabet. Bonet's book is considered the forefather of phonetic and speech therapy prevalent in modern educational practice.

More than a century after the publication of Bonet's treatise, his ideas were taken up by Charles-Michel de l'Épée, a French clergyman and philanthropist. De l'Épée had trained as a Catholic priest but devoted most of his life to helping the poor of Paris. Legend has it that on one of his regular missions into the vast Parisian slums, he came across two deaf sisters and was enthralled to see them communicating effectively with each other by sign language. He founded the world's first free school for the deaf in Paris in 1760, a flagship institution that went on to become the highly influential Institut National de Jeunes Sourds de Paris and inspired similar projects and affiliated schools across Europe.

Although Charles-Michel de l'Épée is often cited as the inventor of French sign language, or at least the man who taught the deaf of Paris to use sign language, the deaf community of Paris had in fact been using an informal system of communication signals – sometimes referred to as Old Signed French – for several centuries. De l'Épée's contribution was to develop and adapt this practice into a coherent formalized language, by adding grammatical elements and gestures to convey concepts rather than merely alphabetical representations, and his legacy in deaf education is considerable. Reverend Thomas Hopkins Gallaudet, an American clergyman, visited one of de l'Épée's schools in the early nineteenth century and returned to the USA with one of its former pupils, Laurent Clerc, to found the American School for the Deaf at Hartford, Connecticut. His son, Edward Miner Gallaudet, later founded what would become Gallaudet University for the deaf in Washington, D.C. These institutions helped to establish American Sign Language, which incorporated many elements of the de l'Épée system.

Sign language suffered something of a setback in the late nineteenth century when a movement of non-deaf educators opposed to manual languages began arguing vociferously for an 'oralist' approach, which focused on lip-reading and speech therapy. They believed that sign language hindered the deaf community and prevented students from mastering the language used by their parents and peers. Manualists such as Edward Miner Gallaudet argued passionately for the effectiveness of sign language, but for almost a century the oralists prevailed.

In the 1970s, damning reports revealed the ineffectiveness of the oralist approach, and the pioneering work of Dr William C. Stokoe at Gallaudet University demonstrated that sign language possessed enough features to be considered a language in its own right. Since then, signing has regained its respectability around the world. It has been reintroduced into schools, and now appears on television and at theatre performances, while still retaining its diverse national, and in some cases even regional, variations.

Alexander Graham Bell and the Oralism Movement

Alexander Graham Bell is best known as a revered scientist, engineer and the inventor of the telephone, but he was also an ardent advocate of the oralism movement in deaf education, which maintained that sign language was counterproductive.

Bell's father, Alexander Melville Bell, had been the creator of the Visible Speech method of phonetic notation, which tracked the position of the lips, tongue and throat in producing speech sounds. Bell Sr's method was originally designed to teach correct elocution – a Victorian obsession – and was used to teach the deaf community to speak. Alexander Graham Bell was convinced that, by teaching speech through his father's methods alongside lip-reading practices, deafness could be eradicated.

In 1872 Bell opened the School of Vocal Physiology and Mechanics of Speech in Boston with a view to promoting his father's teaching methods, which he did with considerable popularity and success. He also taught as a private tutor, his most famous pupil being the writer and political activist Helen Keller, who later commended Bell on his determination to end the 'inhuman silence which separates and estranges'. Another of his students, Mabel Hubbard, who had been deaf since the age of five and whose father was himself the president of the Clarke School for the Deaf in Massachusetts, subsequently became his wife and the mother of his four children.

Nonetheless the oralist approach is viewed by some historians – and a great many deaf people – as the 'dark ages' of deaf education. Sign language was banned from the classrooms and deaf teachers, experts in manual languages, were gradually replaced by hearing ones. So fervent was the hostility to signing that there are documented cases of deaf pupils having their hands tied behind their backs or to the legs of their chairs to discourage them from communicating by hand. Instead of integrating with hearing society, deaf children lost their own readily understandable language, and signing was inevitably reintroduced as the basis of deaf education and communication.

Hoboglyphs

The term 'hobo' is more commonly used in modern parlance to describe an urban homeless person, but around the start of the twentieth century it referred to an itinerant or nomadic worker who roamed across the United States looking for work wherever it could be found. Hobos travelled across large expanses of the Midwest, usually by jumping on to freight trains that trundled the length and breadth of the country. This favoured mode of travel provides one of the explanations as to the origins of the word 'hobo': an abbreviation of 'hopping boxcars'. Other possible derivations are 'hoe boy', meaning farmhand, or a shortening of 'Houston and Bowery', an area of New York where travelling workers often gathered to find work. Often these travelling vagrants were treated with suspicion and subjected to prejudice and hostility, particularly during the Dust Bowl era of the

Depression, between 1933 and 1936, when a severe drought destroyed thousands of miles of prairie and farmland. Approximately 500,000 people were left homeless by the catastrophic dust storms that ravaged the Great Plains, causing crops to fail and farms to be repossessed, and forcing many thousands to migrate to look for work.

Hobo markings, such as these ones near the Mississippi River in New Orleans, communicate to other migrant workers where food and shelter might be found

In the face of severe hardship, the migrant workers developed a secret sign language known as hoboglyphs, consisting of a set of symbols that could be scratched or chalked on to fence posts, buildings, telegraph poles, gates or road signs. The symbols were messages to other travellers giving information on the best places to camp or find a meal, the possibility of finding work, or the dangers that might lie ahead. The markings comprised combinations of simple shapes (circles, squares and triangles), abstract lines, basic images, numbers and squiggles and arrows. The arrows provided geographical directions while the shapes provided cryptic messages and warnings. For example, a rectangle with a single dot inside denoted danger or hostility to migrant workers, and four horizontal slashes and the number 18 meant it was possible to get food in exchange for a day's work. This unique system of symbols was used to keep the community of travelling workers safe, fed and in work, and was simple enough in its design to appear random to the untrained eye.

After the Second World War, the practice of marking hoboglyphs gradually died out, largely due to a period of relative economic prosperity, while a growth in the number and size of major cities caused a sharp decline in the number of migrant workers travelling across the country looking for employment.

How the Hobo Code
Inspired *Mad Men*

Hoboglyphs inspired an episode of the acclaimed television drama *Mad Men*. In an episode titled 'The Hobo Code', advertising executive Don Draper undergoes a marijuana-induced flashback at a party and remembers an incident from his childhood on a Depression-era farmstead. A travelling hobo arrives looking for work and Draper's stepmother agrees to provide food and shelter in return for the man doing some chores. The young Don befriends the hobo, who he discovers hails from New York and has chosen to be a hobo in order to be free to roam the country, and Don tells him that his real mother was a prostitute and that his father is abusive. The hobo explains the hobo code, showing Don what the various symbols mean; the following morning, after the hobo has left, Don discovers the image of a knife has been drawn on the Drapers' gate, denoting to other travellers that the owner of the house is untrustworthy and dangerous. The encounter is Don's initiation into the power of symbols to communicate ideas or messages – a valuable asset in the cut-throat world of advertising that he and his fellow 'Mad Men' inhabit.

PART FIVE

Symbols of the Present and the Future

'Beyond the edge of the world there's a space where emptiness and substance neatly overlap, where past and future form a continuous, endless loop. And, hovering about, there are signs no one has ever read, chords no one has ever heard.'

Haruki Murakami

Rapid advances in communications technology over the past thirty years have led to the creation and adoption of a new language of signs and symbols. The use of emails, mobile phones, text messaging and social network sites has increasingly led to a rise in the practicality of abbreviations, symbols and shorthand in conventional written – and verbal – communication.

What will the signs and symbols of the future be? Will formal language continue to recede in favour of the expediency of speed, brevity and 'user-friendliness'? If so – that is, if we embrace technology and the possibilities it offers for expanding the margins of human communication across traditional boundaries of language and culture – an increase in universally understood signs and symbols will not only be inevitable, but also vital.

The 'At' Symbol

The @ symbol has become the key motif of contemporary electronic communication, thanks largely to its use in email addresses, social media 'handles' (user names, such as on Twitter), and in text-message shorthand. Indeed the @ has become so important in modern life that a large printed representation of it – created by computer scientist Ray Tomlinson in 1971 – was proudly acquired for permanent display at New York's Museum of Modern Art in 2010. But the origins of the symbol are somewhat contentious, and, perhaps most surprising of all, it has no official name and is known by various different names across the world.

We do know that the @ symbol was used in medieval merchants' letters and monastic manuscripts prior to the invention of the printing press, but its genesis may well have been much earlier. American palaeographer Berthold Louis Ullman, in his book *Ancient Writing and its Influence*, describes how monks, faced with the arduous and seemingly endless task of making multiple copies of classical Latin texts, naturally looked for shortcuts. He proposes that the @ symbol was an abbreviation of the Latin word *ad* (meaning 'towards' or 'to') and was formed by adding an elegant tail to the *a* character to signify the *d*, although other scholars have noted that such lazy practice by holy scribes, if it existed at all, would be in contravention of the monastic code of patience, diligence and fortitude, and furthermore that the use of specific ligatures to abbreviate words followed strict conventions (see Ampersand, p.194).

Nowadays more commonly associated with social networking sites, this very early use of the @ symbol is from the fourteenth-century Bulgarian translation of a popular Byzantine chronicle

One of the earliest surviving uses of the symbol is in a letter by an Italian wine merchant, Francesco Lapi, which was sent from Seville to Rome on 4 May 1536. In the letter, Lapi lists the current prices of wine, presumably for exportation purposes, and uses the @ sign to denote an amphora, the large clay pots in which wine was traditionally transported. In the intervening centuries the symbol came to be used by traders and merchants to denote the rate or price of individual units of a particular product, e.g. 12 oranges @ $0.50, and became commonplace in sales ledgers and accounting practices.

The @ did not appear on the early commercial typewriters on sale from the 1870s onwards, and its use in accounting declined in the later half of the twentieth century. The symbol might well have become obsolete – an occasional obscure button on later typewriter keyboards – had it not been for Ray Tomlinson's artwork, @, at MOMA. It was while working on an early prototype of an intranet system that Tomlinson decided to give new life to the anachronistic @ symbol on the keyboard of his Teletype Model 33 by employing it as a means of separating different recipients' names. Before long the first electronic messages were being passed between computers in Tomlinson's office using his new addressing system, and the symbol has of course gone on to become the standard method of distinguishing electronic and online identities.

The Sign With No Name

The @ symbol is informally referred to as 'the at sign' in English but it has no official title. As a result of the unusual anonymity of this ubiquitous symbol, it has a variety of nicknames around the world, most of them relating to animals. Here are some of its more inventive monikers:

apenstaartje: Dutch for 'monkey's tail'
ludo a: Bosnian for 'crazy a'
snabela: Danish for 'elephant's-trunk a'
kissanhnta: Finnish for 'cat's tail'
klammeraffe: German for 'spider monkey'
papaki: Greek for 'little duck'
shtrudel: Hebrew for 'strudel'
kukac: Hungarian for 'worm'
dalphaengi: Korean for 'snail'
grisehale: Norwegian for 'pig's tail'
sobachka: Russian for 'little dog'

The Ampersand

The & ('and') sign, known as the ampersand, is another symbol that has taken on a second life in the modern age through being widely used in computing. The origins of the ampersand can be traced back as far as the first century AD, when it was used as a scribal ligature, or shortcut, in laboriously hand-copied Latin manuscripts. The symbol was formed by running the letters *e* and *t* together in one flowing stroke to represent the word *et*, Latin for 'and'.

The *et* ligature might have died an early death had it not been for an eighth-century English scholar named Alcuin of York – 'the most learned man anywhere to be found', according to the contemporary historian Einhard – who in 782 was invited by the Emperor Charlemagne to teach at the Palace of Aachen and was subsequently asked by him to devise a standardized style for writing Latin script across his sprawling empire. Alcuin's work at Charlemagne's 'scriptorium' led to the development of the calligraphic script known as Carolingian minuscule, which prevailed for four centuries. It eschewed a lot of the common Latin ligatures but kept the *et* ligature, which over time became more stylized to resemble the ampersand found on modern keyboards.

Gutenberg's invention of the printing press in around 1450 led to widespread use of the ampersand in printed books, and for some time in the nineteenth century it was considered the unofficial twenty-seventh letter of the English alphabet, following *Z* in classroom recitations. Indeed, it is this usage that gave the symbol its name. Children were taught to recite letters that in themselves formed a word as, for instance, 'I *per se* [of itself is] I' and 'A *per se* A'; likewise & was called out as 'and *per se* and', a slurred version of which became 'ampersand'.

From the late nineteenth century onwards, the use of the ampersand in printed scripts began to decline and was used mainly in commercial signwriting. The advent of the computer age has given this once-elegant abbreviation a new series of functions through its use in programming languages and text-messaging shorthand. It is this latter use that seems the most pertinent: just as monastic scribes looked for ways to speed up the toils of their labour, the pace of modern communication has provided a renewed need for the time-saving ampersand.

The Bluetooth Symbol

Perhaps unbelievably, the distinctive symbol for the Bluetooth wireless data system interface, which is prevalent on the screens of countless electronic communication devices the world over, has its origins in the exploits of a medieval Scandinavian warrior king.

Harald Gormsson succeeded his father Gorm the Old as king of what is now Denmark in AD 958. In keeping with medieval historians' penchant for ascribing mildly insulting epithets to their monarchs, Harald is referred to in several Norse chronicles as Blátand (Bluetooth), on account of having badly stained teeth. Legend has it that Harald was particularly fond of the wild blueberries that grew in abundance in Denmark, hence his dental discolouring.

Harald Bluetooth is credited with erecting two large carved rune stones on the burial mounds of his mother and father close to the town of Jelling. The Jelling Stones, one of the most famous heritage sites in Denmark, hold UNESCO World Heritage status thanks to their significance as a bridge between the rituals of Scandinavian paganism and the spread of Christianity under Harald Bluetooth. The larger of the two stones features a depiction of Jesus alongside references to Harald's achievements in uniting Denmark and Norway by quelling the warring factions and tribes.

In 1994, Swedish electronics company Ericsson proposed the creation of a wireless interface system that would allow the world's rapidly increasing number of mobile communications devices to link up and share data over short distances, without the use of cables. To this end Ericsson invited several of their competitors in the electronic communications field to form a Special Interest Group (SIG), with a view to collaborating on the project. During preliminary meetings between the companies, Ericsson engineer Sven Mathesson gave Intel programmer Jim Kardach a copy of Frans Gunnar Bengtsson's *The Long Ships*, a bestselling historical novel set in the court of Harold Bluetooth, as a gift. Kardach saw a number of symbolic similarities between the ancient king's quest for unity in the face of division and the unifying goals of the SIG, and so the project was given the working title 'Bluetooth'.

In honour of the spirit of collaboration inspired by

Harald Bluetooth, the interface's logo was designed to incorporate the king's initials (H and B) in the Scandinavian runic alphabet.

Apple Mac Command Symbol

Like the Bluetooth symbol, the unusual square-with-looping-corners symbol that is particular to Apple Mac computer keyboards also has its origins in Scandinavia. The development team behind early-1980s Mac computers came up with the idea of adding a command key to a standard keyboard, which, when used in combination with other keys, could provide a shortcut to an array of menu commands. Originally the key was designed, naturally enough, with the famous Apple logo on it, but Steve Jobs felt that this was laziness on the part of the design team and that his now-world-famous icon was being overused. The job of redesigning the symbol fell to a graphic artist named Susan Kare, who looked through countless directories of international symbols before happening across an obscure sign common on campsites in Sweden and other parts of Scandinavia, where information boards use the sign to denote a 'place of interest', such as a waterfall or other natural phenomenon. Jobs liked the idea of the sign directing users to 'places of interest' on the computer and the symbol has remained an ever-present and unique feature of Apple keyboards.

The Power and Standby Signs

The circle-and-line figure indicating the power or standby switch on an electrical product has been commonplace since it was standardized by the International Electrotechnical Commission in 1973, but it had been in informal use for a number of decades before that.

Early electronic equipment had switches with 'on' and 'off' states, much like a common light switch, which evolved to binary '1' and '0' as the need to bypass language barriers arose. The advent of a single button to perform both functions, as on modern-day computers and mobile phones, led to the '1' being moved inside the '0' to create the power sign. The development of 'standby' mode in televisions and computers necessitated a variation on this symbol, with the

'1' dissecting the '0' instead of being contained within it.

The standby mode symbol has become unexpectedly iconic among technology enthusiasts and has been used in logos for various technology and office-supplies companies; it even for a time adorned fashionable T-shirts much as the smiley face had done. But arguably its most ingenious modern usage has been well outside the world of computer technology. In 2010 the standby symbol defeated nearly 600 other hopefuls in a competition to design the wrappers for New York City-branded condoms. The other five finalists included a top hat, a municipal manhole cover and even a suggestive train tunnel.

'I hope my design reminds people they are in control,' said creator Luis Acosta, whose design now adorns millions of condom packets distributed free throughout the city.

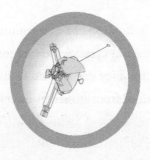

The Pioneer Plaque

The Pioneer plaque was designed by American astronomers Carl Sagan and Frank Drake to accompany the launch of the Jupiter-bound *Pioneer 10* exploratory spacecraft in February 1972. An identical plaque was also fixed to *Pioneer 11* just over a year later. The plaque is, to date, mankind's only attempt to communicate *symbolically* with an alien culture – for whom, of course, our universal visual constants of shape, colour and form might not hold. It is also the only man-made diagram to have gone beyond our solar system.

Dr Sagan was enthusiastic about the idea of a message on the *Pioneer* spacecraft and enlisted Dr Drake (creator of the 'Drake Equation', a method to estimate the number of alien civilizations present in the Milky Way) to help design a plaque, in collaboration with his own wife, Linda Salzman Sagan, who prepared the artwork. The eventual design was etched into two gold-anodized aluminium plates roughly the size of tablet computers, which were attached to the antenna support struts of the spacecraft in a position where they could be shielded from erosion by interstellar space dust.

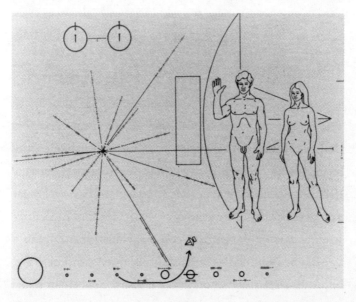

The Pioneer plaque was designed to communicate with our extraterrestrial neighbours, although it also sparked fears of imminent alien invasion

The Pioneer plaque has since been superseded by vastly more complex and purposeful communication attempts and was perhaps never really meant as a potential form of communication with extraterrestrial life but rather as a celebration of the fact that, at the time, the *Pioneer* crafts were the most distant objects sent from Earth. Thus the plaque, hastily created by people who were given a very limited timeframe in which to create a symbolic message, has became iconic more for what it reveals about us than as a coherent symbolic message to be puzzled over by bug-eyed aliens.

The first and main problem Sagan and Drake encountered was how to communicate with a culture with which we share no graphical parameters. Even supposing that extraterrestrials have a visual cortex and 'see' things in the same spectrum as ourselves, we cannot assume that the sea, land or sun they may be familiar with bear any great relation to our own – and this is before we speculate as to the extraterrestrials' size, form or ability to understand doodles from a far-flung galaxy. There are, however, certain constants in the universe that can be relied upon to have some ubiquity – at least in space terms – in what may be deemed 'our local vicinity': factors such as the prevalence and attributes of hydrogen, the placement of stars in relation to us and the universal mathematical constants governing the way the universe operates. Pi, for instance, cannot be anything but pi regardless of how it is notated.

The design of the plaque itself comprises a series of simple diagrams including schematic representations of scientific formulas, a map of our solar system and the proposed trajectory of the *Pioneer* spacecraft, and two human figures of a man and woman – the latter, of course, causing the most controversy. The man's hand is raised in a manner that resembles waving and the woman stands beside him, her head slightly inclined or perhaps looking at him. Both are implicitly naked. The male's genitals are exposed but the female figure has no genital cleft and neither figure has any pubic hair. To avoid offending sensitive readers at the time, some newspapers reprinting the image removed all signs of genitalia as well as the woman's nipples. Further objections came from feminists who claimed that the woman's poise was markedly subservient (which it is), from civil rights activists who claimed both figures were disproportionately Caucasian (which they are) and from various alarmists and conspiracy theorists who claimed that the plaque, by advertising our whereabouts, might lead to a hostile invasion of Earth.

The representative images of two humans are the most recognizable symbol from our own perspective but ironically might be the most meaningless part of the whole message for any potential recipient. Even accepting the hypothetical notion that alien beings are able to distinguish the figures as distinct life forms, they may well misinterpret the raised hand as a threat or a declaration of hostile intent.

By far the more interesting part of the message lies in the thought given to finding universal constants from which a level of communication might be derived. Hydrogen, the most abundant element in the universe, is represented by two circular symbols joined by a binary '1' – a diagram that, if correctly interpreted by our extraterrestrial counterparts and used as a key to the other diagrams on the plaque, actually conveys a fairly accurate idea of how far from its source the craft has travelled and the length of time it has been travelling, even if it has been drifting in space for millions of years.

An additional diagram in the form of a radial pattern indicates the relative position of the solar system to notable space landmarks, although the schematic diagram of our solar system might actually serve to throw any recipient off the scent somewhat, given radical advances in our astronomical understanding since 1972: Pluto has been demoted from planet to dwarf planet and fainter rings have been discovered around Neptune, Uranus and Jupiter.

Although the plaque is symbolically interesting, not least as a reflection of the times in which it was created, it will have little hope of ever reaching the bug eyes for which it was half-heartedly intended. As is often the case when considering the vast expanses of space, there is a general public misconception of the times and distances involved. *Pioneer 10*, at time of writing, is currently beyond the orbit of Pluto at the edge of our solar system and heading towards the Aldebaran system (in the constellation Taurus), although it is not expected to arrive for another two million years. The scales involved are so enormous that, for the next century, if a passing spaceship were to pick it up, *Pioneer* would still be far closer to our system than to any other – the equivalent of finding a message in a bottle just after it has been thrown into the waves.

The Pioneer 'Controversy'

Widespread objections to the Pioneer plaque ranged from the cogent feminist argument to the wild-eyed panic of the invasion-fearing isolationists. But by far the most amusing protestations came, as usual, from the prudes and armchair moralists who fired off letters to various national newspapers, such as this one, which appeared in the *Los Angeles Times*:

I must say I was shocked by the blatant display of both male and female sex organs on the front page of the *Times*. Surely this form of sexual exploitation is below the standards our community has come to expect from the *Times*. Isn't it enough that we must tolerate the bombardment of pornography through the medium of film and smut magazines? Isn't it bad enough that our own space agency officials have found it necessary to spread this filth even beyond our own solar system?

This was followed some days later by this excellent riposte:

I certainly agree with those people protesting our sending those dirty pictures of naked people out into space. I think the way it should have been done is to visually bleep out the reproductive organs of the drawings of the man and the woman. Next to them we should have had a stork carrying a little bundle from heaven. Then if we really want our celestial neighbours to know how far we have progressed intellectually, we should have included pictures of Santa Claus, the Easter Bunny and the Tooth Fairy.

Selected Bibliography

Appiah, K.A. and Gates, H.L., ed., *The Dictionary of Global Culture*, Penguin 1996

Chevelier, Jean and Gheerbrant, Alain, *The Penguin Dictionary of Symbols* (trans Buchan Brown, J.), Penguin 1996

Cirlot, J.C., *Dictionary of Symbols*, Routledge 1983

Cooper, J.C., *An Illustrated Encyclopaedia of Traditional Symbols*, Thames & Hudson 1979

Gauding, Madonna, *The Signs and Symbols Bible*, Godsfield Press 2009

Nozedar, Adele, *The Illustrated Signs and Symbols Sourcebook*, Harper Collins 2010

Wilkinson, K., ed., Signs And Symbols, Dorsley Kingsley 2008

Various, *The Book of Symbols*, Taschen GmbH 2010

Picture Acknowledgements

Prehistoric cave painting 23; Rosetta Stone 34; royal coat of arms 42; fleur-de-lys p.51, Action Sports Photography; yin and yang 61; anti-Semitic clothing badge 67; Sacred Heart of Jesus 70; New York loves me p.72, dutourdumonde; Buddhist swastika p.76, Attila JANDI; Nazi swastika p.77, Neftali; Romanian stamp p.85, Kiev.Victor; shamrock streetlamp 90; skull and crossbones in Buenos Aires 96; peace signs p.100, Emine Dursun; Olympic torch p.107, kycstudio/iStockphoto; Olympic rings p.108, meunierd/Shutterstock.com; smiley postage stamp p.115, catwalker; Scottish pound p.127, Ruth Black; Jason and the Argonauts 149; Fire insurance mark 154; Route 66 164; roadworks sign 167; Harry Beck Tube map p.171, Neftali; Sign Language Plaque 174; Hoboglyphs 181; Byzantine manuscript 191; Pioneer Plaque 203

All other illustrations from www.shutterstock.com

Acknowledgements

I should like to proffer my heartfelt thanks to the following people for their invaluable help, advice and support (both physically and symbolically) in the conception of this book: Dr Tim McIlwaine for his excellent additional research and supplementary material, Mathew Clayton for helping to get the project off the ground, Silvia Compton and Gabriella Nemeth for their judicious and sympathetic editing skills, Kate Truman for her invaluable proofreading, R. Lucas and J. Fleet and the staff at Sussex University Library, the design and production team at Michael O'Mara Books and my family and friends for their patience and encouragement.

INDEX

INDEX

INDEX